Otterburn 1388

Bloody border conflict

Campaign • 164

Otterburn 1388

Bloody border conflict

Peter Armstrong • Illustrated by Stephen Walsh

First published in Great Britain in 2006 by Osprey Publishing,
Midland House, West Way, Botley, Oxford OX2 0PH, UK
443 Park Avenue South, New York, NY 10016, USA
E-mail: info@ospreypublishing.com

A CIP catalogue record for this book is available from the British Library

ISBN 1 84176 980 0

Design: The Black Spot
Index by Alison Worthington
Maps by The Map Studio
3D bird's-eye views by HL Studios
Originated by PPS Grasmere, Leeds, UK
Printed in China through World Print Ltd.

06 07 08 09 10   10 9 8 7 6 5 4 3 2 1

For a catalogue of all books published by Osprey please contact:

NORTH AMERICA
Osprey Direct, C/o Random House Distribution Center, 400 Hahn Road,
Westminster, MD 21157, USA
E-mail: info@ospreydirect.com

ALL OTHER REGIONS
Osprey Direct UK, P.O. Box 140, Wellingborough, Northants, NN8 2FA, UK
E-mail: info@ospreydirect.co.uk

www.ospreypublishing.com

Artist's note

Readers may care to note that the original paintings from
which the colour plates in this book were prepared are
available for private sale. All reproduction copyright
whatsoever is retained by the Publishers. All enquiries should
be addressed to:

Stephen Walsh
11 Longacre Street
Macclesfield
Cheshire SK10 1AY
UK
www.stephenwalsh.co.uk

The Publishers regret that they can enter into no
correspondence upon this matter.

Key to military symbols

XXXXX	XXXX	XXX	XX	X	III	II
Army Group	Army	Corps	Division	Brigade	Regiment	Battalion

I				Key to unit identification		
Company/Battery	Infantry	Artillery	Cavalry			

Key to unit identification

Unit identifier — Parent unit
Commander
(+) with added elements
(-) less elements

CONTENTS

ORIGINS OF THE CAMPAIGN   7
Anglo-Scottish relations 1329–88

CHRONOLOGY   14

OPPOSING COMMANDERS   16
Scottish commanders • English commanders

OPPOSING ARMIES   22
The Scottish army • The English army • Orders of battle

OPPOSING PLANS   31
Scottish plans • English plans

THE CAMPAIGN OF 1388   34
The Scots muster in the Forest of Jedburgh • The earl of Fife invades the West March
The earl of Douglas invades the East March • The Scots at the gates of Newcastle
The Scots withdraw to Otterburn • Hotspur pursues the Scots • The Scots at Otterburn

THE BATTLE OF OTTERBURN, AUGUST 1388   51
Medieval written sources • The site of the battle of Otterburn
The date of the battle of Otterburn • The Scots fortify themselves at Otterburn
The earl of Douglas counter-attacks • The earl of March tips the scales
Success of the English left wing

AFTERMATH   71
Death of the earl of Douglas • The bishop of Durham makes a poor showing
Casualties and captives of Otterburn • The situation in Scotland after Otterburn

THE BATTLE OF HUMBLETON HILL, 14 SEPTEMBER 1402   81
Scotland, 1389–1402

EPILOGUE   90

THE BATTLEFIELDS TODAY   92

SELECT BIBLIOGRAPHY   94

INDEX   95

Earl of Angus

Earl of Strathearn

Earl of Buchan

Earl of Carrick

Earl of Sutherland

Earl of Caithness

Earl of Ross

Earl of Fife

Royal Arms of Scotland

Earl of Moray

Earl of Atholl

Earl of Mar

Earl of Lennox

R O S S

Moray Firth

Inverness

B U C H A N

Loch Ness

M O R A Y

Strathspey

S C O T L A N D

M A R

A T H O L L

A N G U S

Perth

Firth of Tay

STRATHEARN

MENTEITH

FIFE

Argyll

Loch Lomond

LENNOX

Stirling

Firth of Forth

Dunbar

Rothesay

Bute

Glasgow

Edinburgh

Dalkeith

Fast Castle

Kintyre

Arran

Firth of Clyde

Clyde

Lothian

M A R C H

The Merse

Berwick-upon-Tweed

Dundonald

Tweed

Roxburgh (1460)

Tweed

Ayr

CARRICK

Nithsdale

Teviot

Jedburgh (1409)

Cheviot Hills

Alnwick

N

Annandale

Northumberland

0   20 miles

0   20km

G a l l o w a y

Dumfries

Lochmaben (1384)

Threave Castle

Carlisle

E N G L A N D

Solway Firth

Tyne

Cumberland

- - - - - Area ceded by Edward Balliol to Edward III in 1332

- · - · - Anglo-Scottish border

Scottish castles in English hands with dates of their fall

ORIGINS OF THE CAMPAIGN

ANGLO-SCOTTISH RELATIONS 1329–88

Robert Bruce's great victory over the English at Bannockburn in 1314 loosened the grasp of Scotland's rapacious southern neighbour on the Northern Kingdom. Despite the magnitude of their defeat, the English refused to acknowledge Bruce as King of Scots or to recognize Scottish independence. In the years that followed Bannockburn, Scotland's hard-won military ascendancy allowed King Robert to unleash the destructive power of the Scots on the north of England in an attempt to force Edward II of England to conclude a peace that would not only recognize Robert as King of Scots but also acknowledge Scottish independence. The depredations of the Scots caused widespread devastation and ruined the economy of large areas of the northern counties, which were reduced to a pitiful condition. Despite the repeated harrying and spoliation of the north, Edward II remained indifferent to its plight. By 1327, Robert Bruce was worn out and ill, and though he was only 52 he was approaching the end of his life. His only legitimate son, David, who was to be his successor to the throne of Scotland, was still a three-year-old child. King Robert's aggressive policy towards England had not brought results and his aims seemed as far from being achieved as ever. Then, unexpectedly, events in England took a turn favourable to the Scots. In January 1327 the hapless and increasingly unpopular Edward II was deposed and his 14-year-old son was crowned in his place as Edward III on 1 February. A council of regency was established, dominated by Isabella the Queen Mother and her lover Mortimer, whose all-pervading influence corrupted the unpopular regime. The ailing King Robert responded to the situation in the south with a renewed onslaught on the northern counties of England. A disastrous and costly campaign in

The early phase of the Scottish Wars of Independence took place during the reigns of John Balliol (1292–96) and Robert I (1306–29). Their equestrian seals display the Royal Arms of Scotland, which symbolize the nation's strength and independence. The lion rampant of Scotland was first used by William 'the Lion' (1143–1214). His son, Alexander II (1214–49), added a bordure of fleurs-de-lis. The double tressure flory-counter-flory was first used on the great seal of Alexander III in 1251. (Author's drawings)

Weardale in July failed to dislodge the Scots, who not only continued to hold much of Northumberland, but began to take possession of their conquests by parcelling out land there on a permanent basis. Isabella and Mortimer realized they had to act but, knowing that the backlash of defeat would bring about their downfall, chose not to risk renewing the war against the Scots but to make peace. By the Treaty of Edinburgh that followed in 1328, England renounced her claim to sovereignty over Scotland, which settled the question of Scottish independence. The treaty marked the conclusion of the long, damaging war that had first flared up in 1296. Robert Bruce's aggressive policy towards England had succeeded and set a precedent for generations of succeeding Scottish policymakers. Yet it was all for nothing; the peace that followed did not long outlive King Robert himself who died, in June 1329 at the age of 54, worn out and racked by illness. His legacy of achievement would not be matched by his successors to the throne of Scotland. He was succeeded by his seven-year-old son David, who was crowned at Scone in November 1331 as King David II. The ensuing festivities proved to be the high water mark of Scottish fortunes in the Wars of Independence, for a new and disastrous phase was about to begin.

In 1330 Edward III overthrew Mortimer in a palace coup at Nottingham and took control of the government himself. Though he was not yet 18, he was cast in the mould of his grand-father Edward I, the 'hammer of the Scots'. He was resentful of the Treaty of Edinburgh and burned for vengeance for the humiliation of his father at Bannockburn and for the recent fiasco in Weardale. In 1332 Edward covertly sponsored an audacious private invasion of Scotland by a group of self-seeking adventurers who had been disinherited by Robert Bruce and who sought to regain their inheritance by force of arms. They were led by Edward Balliol, son of John Balliol, King of Scots, whom Edward I had deposed in 1296. With scant regard for Scotland's independence he paid homage to Edward III for his kingdom before his expedition sailed. An extraordinary victory at Dupplin Muir, outside Perth, resulted in Balliol gaining the crown of Scotland, and, though he was ejected from the country by the end of the year, he was returned to power in 1333 after Edward III's victory over the Scots at Hallidon Hill beside Berwick. The tide had turned, the short-lived military supremacy of the Scots was gone; the day of the English long-bowman had dawned.

The price of Edward's support of Balliol was high; in addition to paying homage for his kingdom to Edward he was forced to cede permanently large areas of southern Scotland to England. David II took refuge in France where Philip VI, obliged by the 'auld alliance' between France and Scotland, provided a safe haven for the young king. It was not until 1341 that the situation in Scotland allowed him to return home. The 'auld alliance' with France, which was initiated in 1326 by the Treaty of Corbeil, was the cornerstone of Scottish foreign policy until the Reformation. It was a lopsided arrangement, which obliged the Scots to intervene in any Anglo-French conflict but was without a reciprocal agreement; French obligations were ambiguous, though they promised French support and an end to Scottish isolation in European affairs. It

Edward Balliol's return to power in 1333 was short lived, and his authority and the territory over which he held sway rapidly diminished. In 1356 he resigned his crown and retired to Yorkshire where he died in obscurity in 1364. For a time there were two kings of Scotland as Balliol's reign overlapped that of David Bruce. (Author's illustration; McGarrigle Collection)

was an arrangement calculated to sour relations with England and left the two countries locked in a cycle of hostile truces and occasional outbreaks of open warfare.

In 1346, Edward III was in France with the main English army when David II, in support of the French, invaded England and was heavily defeated and captured at Neville's Cross outside Durham. He was a prisoner of Edward III until 1357, when he was released on a huge ransom of 100,000 marks; the 'auld alliance' had cost Scotland dear.

Despite such setbacks as the disaster of Neville's Cross, which resulted in the loss of large areas of the Borders, the Scots steadily eroded the English position in southern Scotland. However the recapture, by the Scots, of the town of Berwick-upon-Tweed in 1355 was a step too far and brought retribution the following year, when Edward III led an army into the south-east of Scotland that caused widespread devastation, long remembered as the 'Burnt Candlemas' campaign. It was a lesson to the Scots who, though they continued to abrade the English position, were wary of provoking massive retaliation, which could wipe out their gains at a single blow. When David II agreed a 14-year truce with Edward III in 1369, large areas of the Scottish border region were still under English control, including parts of Annandale, Teviotdale, lower Tweeddale, Berwickshire and the strongholds of Berwick, Roxburgh, Jedburgh and Lochmaben. This situation continued to the end of David's reign and into the early years of his successor, Robert II, though the important castle of Lochmaben fell to the Scots in February 1384. The long truce had expired at the beginning of that month and a period of sporadic warfare ensued, typified by raid and counter-raid, so characteristic of military activity on the Anglo-Scottish frontier.

In 1385, a force under the Admiral of France, Jean de Vienne, landed in Scotland as part of an ambitious French plan to attack England from the north and south simultaneously, though this came to nothing. English reaction to this threat was immediate, in the form of one of the largest armies ever assembled in the course of the Hundred Years War, which Richard II led in person into Scotland as far as Edinburgh. The invasion force cut a swathe of destruction across south-eastern Scotland but the Franco-Scottish forces declined battle and, in time-honoured fashion, withdrew beyond the Forth. The French, finding co-operation with the Scots impossible, went home. Richard II, having achieved nothing at great expense, withdrew from Scotland, leaving the Scots once more with an opportunity to raid northern England before a further truce came into effect towards the end of October that year; it was a familiar pattern of events. On the expiry in turn of this truce, on 19 June 1388, the Scottish government did not seek to renew it. It was a decision that they knew would lead inevitably to war.

Several factors may have influenced this course of action; the Scots probably sought to take advantage of the unstable political situation in England brought about by the confrontation between the regime of Richard II, and the Lords Appellant, who opposed him. The political situation had only recently escalated into civil war, which had resulted in the defeat of the king's favourite, Robert de Vere, at Radcot Bridge in December, though the crisis ran on into the spring as the so-called 'Merciless Parliament' purged its opponents. The crisis was over by the time the Scots launched their invasion, though they probably thought

The strategically important stronghold of Lochmaben Castle, in Dumfriesshire, guarded the main north–south route up Annandale. The English held it from 1333 to 1384, when Archibald 'the Grim' retook it. Much of the surviving structure belongs to the final decades of English occupation, when major work was carried out to strengthen the defences. (Author's photo)

that the English government would be weakened and distracted by these recent events.

At this time the ascendancy of the Nevilles in the role of defenders of the Marches was usurped by the Percys when Henry Percy (Hotspur), the eldest son of the earl of Northumberland, contracted to replace Sir Ralph Neville as warden of the East March. Froissart certainly knew that there was 'much animosity and hatred between the Percys and Nevilles who were neighbours and had been friends'. His opinion was that: 'The barons and knights of Scotland knowing of this, determined on an

The arms of the powerful families who dominated affairs on the Border in the 14th century still surmount the barbican of the Lucys' ancient fortress at Cockermouth, in Cumbria. From the left they are the arms of: Umfraville, Multon, Lucy, Percy and Neville. In 1368 the castle was in the hands of the Umfravilles but by the 1380s it had passed to the Percys, by the marriage of Maud, the heiress of Anthony de Lucy, and the earl of Northumberland. (Author's illustration)

Alnwick Castle in Northumberland was the seat of the earl of Northumberland. It was acquired by the Percys in 1309 and the defences strengthened throughout the 14th century; by the 1380s it had assumed its present character. (Photo, Keith Durham)

The castle of Carlisle was the main English stronghold of the West March and was in the possession of the Crown. It was besieged nine times by the Scots between 1173 and 1461. The castle was taken only once: in 1216, by Alexander II, who repaired and strengthened it. Since then the castle had proved inviolate to the Scots; even Robert Bruce's all-out attempt to take the town with the help of siege machinery in 1315 failed to reduce the defences. (Author's photo)

inroad into England, as the opportunity was favourable now the English were quarrelling among themselves.'

The success of a Scottish assault on England at this time was further favoured by her renewal of the active war against France. Although delayed by the political climate, an invasion force under the earl of Arundel sailed for France on 10 June. News of his departure must have reached the Scots before they invaded England, and helped persuade them that, with so many English troops abroad, the northern counties of England were wide open to attack.

It has justifiably been said that Prudhoe Castle 'attains more nearly to the ideal of a Border castle than does any other in Northumberland.' The castle occupies a strong site, on a steep spur high above the River Tyne. The Umfravilles built the castle, which passed to the Percys by marriage in 1398. (Author's photo)

The Scots were apprehensive of the possibility of a separate peace between England and France, occasioned by the apparent downturn in France's fortune, which would neglect their interests and leave Scotland vulnerable to the undivided attentions of her southern neighbour. It has been suggested that Scottish strategy in 1388 aimed at the occupation of Cumberland and the capture of the great border fortress of Carlisle, in order to use these to bargain for a favourable peace, though this was a course of action bound to provoke massive retaliation on the part of the English. As events turned out the Scots made little attempt to take Carlisle and, far from occupying the county, they withdrew on learning of Douglas' death at Otterburn after a whirlwind tour of destruction through Cumberland and Westmorland.

Though the Scottish leadership may have pondered the political implications of their decisions, the majority of the fighting men of that aggressive and warlike race would have viewed the forthcoming invasion in terms of the profit that would accrue to them at England's expense. There was military prestige to be gained, and, more tangibly, money from the sale of plundered livestock and goods, and from payments for immunity from the attentions of the raiders such as the £200 that the earl of Douglas himself had recently extracted from the abbey of Holm Cultram. Above all there was money to be gained from the staggering ransoms paid for their lives by the captives brought away by the Scots.

That there was constant rivalry and friction between the houses of Douglas and Percy is undisputed; however there is no evidence, other than Froissart's chivalric notions, to support the popular contention that the battle of Otterburn was the culmination of a long-running feud between these great Border families. The Scottish leadership, headed by Robert II's eldest son, the earl of Carrick, clearly initiated the war of 1388 as an instrument of national policy and the battle was thus an episode in Anglo-Scottish warfare proper rather than the outcome of a family feud. The involvement of the Scottish government is further high-lighted by the participation of the earl of Fife, the king's second surviving son, who led the invasion of the West March, and by that of many of the most prominent Scottish magnates. The scale of the military operations carried out, which included a diversionary attack on Ireland, was well beyond the scope of an individual Scottish lord, however powerful he might be.

The omission of the Scots to renew the truce in June 1388 awakened the English government to the probability of war in the north that summer. Despite recent political upheavals and preoccupation with the French war, they were by no means incapable of putting the defences of the northern Marches in order. No doubt the appointment of Hotspur, who had proved himself both energetic and effective in defence of the Border in recent years as warden of the East March and keeper of Berwick, was part of their preparation for war, as was the appointment early in June of commissioners of array to raise troops for the defence of the Marches. The defensive posture adopted by Hotspur and the northern lords during the early days of the Scottish incursions into the northern counties was due to their orders to await the arrival at Newcastle of the king, who was assembling troops, and the earl of Arundel, who was operating with a fleet in French waters.

CHRONOLOGY

1384

Expiry of long truce between England and Scotland; period of sporadic warfare ensues.

1385

French army in Scotland and combined Franco-Scottish attacks on English border
    fortresses; their ambitious plans against England founder due to an inability to
    cooperate and they leave Scotland in September.
6 Aug Richard II briefly invades Scotland with a large army but the Scots decline battle.

1388

June Scots fail to renew Anglo-Scottish truce, signalling their aggressive intentions.
June(?) Scottish raid on Carlingford in Ireland and the Isle of Man.
27 July The earl of Douglas at Etybredschel, near Selkirk, where he issues a charter to
    Melrose Abbey.
28 July Douglas at Southdean; Scots launch their simultaneous invasions of both the
    East and West Marches of England.
29 July Douglas crosses the Tyne and begins his campaign of destruction in County
    Durham.
30 July Scots skirmish with English troops outside the city of Durham.
31 July Scots in County Durham begin their withdrawal, still causing havoc in the county,
    but moving more slowly now as they are laden with plunder.
1 Aug Scots re-cross the Tyne and make camp before Newcastle.
2 Aug Scots before the walls of Newcastle, Douglas captures Hotspur's 'standard'.
3 Aug Scots before the walls of Newcastle.
    In the West March the Scots are reported near Carlisle.
4 Aug Before dawn the Scots withdraw from Newcastle and ride to Otterburn, where
    they set up a fortified camp.
5 Aug Scots attack Otterburn Tower without success and retire to their camp. Hotspur
    arrives in Redesdale after a long day's march from Newcastle and attacks the Scots;
    battle of Otterburn.
6 Aug Bishop of Durham confronts the Scots at Otterburn; he prudently retires to
    Newcastle.
    News of Otterburn reaches the earl of Fife in the West March, he withdraws to Scotland.
18 Aug Proceedings of a Scottish Council General, held at Linlithgow, record the 'late'
    tenant of Tantallon – James Douglas.

1389

July Scots enter into Anglo-French truce that terminates the Otterburn War.

1390

Death of Robert II, King of Scots; he is succeeded by his son John, Earl of Carrick as
    Robert III.

The earl of Northumberland married Maud, heiress of Anthony de Lucy, a Cumbrian knight, after the death of his first wife Margaret, daughter of Sir Ralf Neville of Raby. The Lucy marriage extended the lands and influence of the Percys immensely and the earl, as part of the arrangement, altered his banner by quartering the blue lion of the Percys with the pike or *lucies* of his new wife. (Author's illustration)

1399

30 Sept Henry Bolingbroke crowned as Henry IV of England in place of the deposed Richard II.

1400

Henry IV invades Scotland.

1402

22 June Combat of Nisbet Muir, earl of March defeats Scots.
14 Sept Battle of Humbleton Hill, Archibald Douglas, 'the Tyneman', defeated.

1403

21 July Battle of Shrewsbury; Hotspur defeated and killed.

1424

17 Aug Archibald Douglas, 'the Tyneman', defeated and killed at the battle of Verneuil.

OPPOSING COMMANDERS

SCOTTISH COMMANDERS

Robert II, King of Scots (1371–90), was the first Stewart king of Scotland; his military experience was limited to an appearance as a young man on the battlefield at Neville's Cross, from which he fled ignominiously without striking a blow. By 1388 'Old Bleary', as he was known, was 71 years of age and living in reclusive retirement at Dundonald Castle; he had little influence on events as the reins of power had slipped from his hands into those of his sons and other unruly and belligerent noblemen.

John Stewart, Earl of Carrick, was the eldest son of Robert II by his first wife, Elizabeth Mure; he had been Guardian of the kingdom since 1384 due to his aged father's incapacity. As Guardian of Scotland he was effectively head of state and in command of the Scottish war effort, though due to his lameness, caused by the kick of a horse, he did not take the field in person. He was overshadowed by his more forceful brother the earl of Fife, who replaced him as Guardian in December 1388. In 1390, on the death of his father, John assumed the title Robert III, because his own name was associated with defeat. He was by his own account 'the worst of Kings and the most miserable of men'; he died in 1406 to be succeeded by his 12-year-old son as James I.

Perched high on its rocky eminence, the forbidding castle of the Stewarts dominates the picturesque Ayrshire village of Dundonald. In his later years King Robert II made the castle his retreat from worldly affairs, and it was here that he died in 1390. (Author's photo)

Robert Stewart, Earl of Fife and Menteith, third son of Robert II by Elizabeth Mure, became earl of Fife by agreement with Isabella of Fife, widow of his elder brother Walter who died in 1362. He led the invasion of the West March of England in person and was effectively overall commander of Scottish forces during the incursions of 1388. He became Duke of Albany in 1398; in 1406, on the death of his brother Robert III, he was appointed Regent, and ruled Scotland until his death in 1420. Fife was an experienced commander and had led a previous invasion of the north of England in 1385.

James, second Earl of Douglas and Mar (*c*.1357–88), was the only son of William, first Earl of Douglas whom he succeeded in 1384. His marriage in 1371 to Isabella Stewart, a daughter of Robert II, ensured that the earldom of Douglas ranked among the highest in Scotland. With the title came regional power and leadership in war, a role that he undertook in 1385 when he led the Scots contingent during the Franco-Scottish invasion of the East March of England. He probably had experience of border warfare from an early age and his record suggests that he was a thoughtful yet bold commander. He was about six years older than his adversary Hotspur, being about 30 years of age when he was killed at Otterburn; he left no legitimate heir.

Sir Archibald Douglas, 'the Grim', Lord of Galloway, was a natural son of 'the Good' Sir James Douglas. Archibald's cognomen 'the Grim' was coined by the English because of his 'terrible countenance in weirfair'. Archibald's power lay in Galloway, where in the 1370s he built mighty Threave Castle as a base and a symbol of Douglas dominance in the south-west of Scotland. He was the most powerful claimant to the title left vacant by the death of James Douglas at Otterburn and became third Earl of Douglas in 1389. He died on Christmas Eve 1400 and was succeeded as fourth Earl of Douglas by his son Archibald, known to posterity as 'the Tyneman', or loser; he was the Scottish commander at Humbleton Hill in 1402, where he was ignominiously defeated by Hotspur and the earl of March.

Sir William Douglas of Nithsdale, in Dumfriesshire, was a natural son of Archibald 'the Grim'. He was a celebrated warrior who, on this account, was given Egidia, the beautiful sister of the earl of Carrick, as his bride. He was a dark-complexioned giant of a man, 'indefatigable in harrying the English'. In 1388 he led the raids on Carlingford, in the north of Ireland, and on the Isle of Man, and on his return was one of the leaders of the invasion of the West March of England. His enmity towards the English led to a duel with Sir Thomas Clifford being arranged in 1390, though it never took place as both travelled to Prussia to take part in a crusade. Ill-feeling between the English and Scots knights led to trouble and in 1391 Douglas was killed on the bridge of Danzig in a fight with a group of English knights, which included Clifford.

George Dunbar, **tenth Earl of Dunbar and third Earl of March** (*c*.1340–1420), is credited in some accounts of the battle with being the real victor of Otterburn rather than the earl of Douglas. His subsequent career not only suggests that this was highly probable but also demonstrates that he was the best Scottish soldier of his time. At Otterburn the timely intervention of his force turned the tide of battle decisively in favour of the Scots. He shifted allegiance to the English about 1400 and fought alongside Hotspur in his victory over the Scots at Humbleton Hill

Archibald 'the Grim' built Threave Castle, following his elevation to the lordship of Galloway in 1369, and it was here that he died on Christmas Eve 1400. The immensely strong tower stands surrounded by a later artillery fortification, on an island in the River Dee, in Kirkcudbrightshire. Recent excavations have shown that the tower was originally part of a much larger complex of buildings. The castle was taken by siege in 1455 and with it fell the Black Douglases. (Author's illustration)

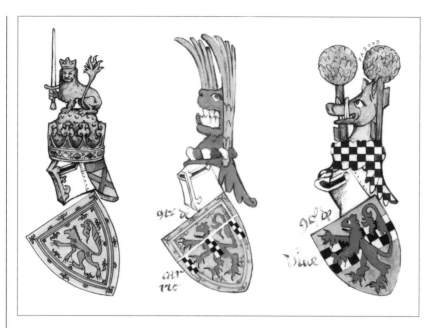

Arms and crests of the Stewarts, from the *Armorial de Gelre* (compiled 1370–95). Left to right: Robert II, King of Scots; John Stewart, Earl of Carrick, who became King Robert III in 1390; Robert Stewart, Earl of Fife and Menteith, created Duke of Albany in 1398. (Author's illustration)

in 1402. In 1403 he was in the service of Henry IV and was instrumental in his defeat of the rebel forces commanded by Hotspur at the battle of Shrewsbury.

John Dunbar, created first Earl of Moray c.1371, was the younger brother of George Dunbar, Earl of March. He fought alongside his brother at Otterburn and later continued the war personally by challenging Thomas Mowbray, Earl of Nottingham, to single combat. A safe-conduct was issued to Moray in March 1390 for his journey to England and the ensuing duel was fought at Smithfield on 28 May. Moray was unhorsed and seriously injured and died as a result at York on his way home in 1391.

Sir Robert Stewart of Durisdeer, in Nithsdale, Dumfriesshire, is referred to by Walter Bower as 'the celebrated knight'. He was associated with Sir William Douglas of Nithsdale as one of the leaders of the expedition to Ireland and the Isle of Man and subsequently of the invasion of the West March of England in 1388. He was a fierce opponent of the English and took every opportunity to fight against them. He fought at Humbleton Hill where he was taken prisoner; the following year, fighting in the retinue of Archibald Douglas, he was killed at the battle of Shrewsbury.

Sir John Swinton, of Swinton, in Berwickshire, was a high-ranking Scots knight, the second husband of Margaret of Mar, mother of James, Earl of Douglas. In the 1370s Sir John had been in English pay and had served in the war in France under the banner of John of Gaunt. His experience must have made him well aware of the danger posed by English archery. His prowess and fame as a soldier were such that he commanded double wages. On his return to Scotland he fought against the English at Otterburn where, according to Walter Bower, the credit for the victory was due in greater measure to Sir John than to the 'dead Douglas'. He was killed, in a manner worthy of a brave and chivalrous knight, at the head of a heroic cavalry charge at Humbleton Hill in 1402.

Arms and crest of James, Earl of Douglas (1357–88), from the contemporary *Armorial de Gelre*. A heart was added to the arms of Douglas after 1330 to commemorate 'the Good' Sir James Douglas, who, in carrying out Robert Bruce's dying wish, that his heart should be carried in battle against the Saracens, was killed by the Moors in Spain. The arms of Douglas are quartered with those of Mar, an earldom that came to James Douglas through his mother, Margaret of Mar. (Author's illustration, after Gelre)

The shattered fragment of masonry that overlooks the picturesque harbour at Dunbar, in East Lothian, is all that remains now of the once mighty castle of the earls of Dunbar and March. The fortunes of the earls themselves have fared no better than their castle; although George Dunbar, who had served Henry IV since 1400, was restored to his former title in 1409, his son lost it once and for all in 1435, when James I enriched himself at the expense of the Dunbars, by confiscating the earldom. (Author's photo)

Sir Mathew Redman, of Levens Hall in Westmorland, governor of Berwick-upon-Tweed. According to Froissart, Sir Mathew fled the field of Otterburn, pursued by Sir James Lindsay of Crawford, who captured him after a fight, an incident that he describes at length. However, there is no other evidence to support this story; Redman, along with Sir Robert Ogle, led the successful attack of the English left wing at Otterburn, and there is evidence that, far from being a prisoner, he was at liberty shortly after the battle. (Author's illustration)

ENGLISH COMMANDERS

Richard II, 'of Bordeaux' (1367–1400), succeeded to the throne of England in 1377, at the age of ten, on the death of his grandfather Edward III. Unlike his famous father, the Black Prince, he was not by nature a military leader, though he was conversant with Anglo-Scottish affairs and led an invasion of Scotland in 1385. Richard lost control of the government to the baronial opposition or 'Lords Appellant' after the battle of Radcot Bridge in December 1387 and did not regain power until May 1389.

Henry Percy (1342–1408) was created first Earl of Northumberland in 1377 in acknowledgement of his prominent role as one of the king's lieutenants in the north. He had fought in the French wars in the 1360s and '70s and was made a Knight of the Garter. He was an able and experienced commander, though he is overshadowed by the fame of his eldest son.

Sir Henry Percy, called 'Hotspur' (1364–1403), was the eldest son of the earl of Northumberland. The fiery spirit and energetic leadership provided by Hotspur in combating Scottish raids into England during the turbulent years on the Border that preceded the battle of Otterburn are thought to have earned him his epithet. In June 1388 he replaced John, Lord Neville as warden of the East March. He was made a Knight of the Garter after Radcot Bridge, as replacement for Robert de Vere, the king's fallen favourite. His cognomen suggests that he was a fiery rather than a thoughtful leader, and his record in the three battles he fought tends to confirm that, though perhaps ideally suited to the raid and counter-raid of border warfare, he was less able as a battlefield commander. His defeat at Otterburn could be attributed to the impetuous and disorganized manner of his attack, though the well-timed intervention in the mêlée of the earl of March was a factor that tipped the scales in favour of the Scots. It was the same earl of March, in English allegiance by 1402, who restrained Hotspur from ordering a headlong charge of his cavalry against the massed ranks of Scots on the heights of Humbleton Hill, and persuaded him of the wisdom of

Alabaster tomb effigy of the baron of Greystoke, in St Andrew's Church, Greystoke, Cumbria. The effigy may be that of Ralph, Baron of Greystoke, who was one of the English leaders at the battle of Humbleton Hill. The style of armour is that of the end of the 14th century rather than that of the early 15th century. Most of the detail has been lost due to centuries of neglect, though enough remains of the monument to show that it was once of the highest quality. In its original state the arms of Greystoke would have been painted on the tight-fitting jupon that covers the body armour. (Author's photo)

employing his archers against such a tempting target. At Shrewsbury, the following year, denied the military talents of March, who had allied himself with Henry IV, Hotspur was defeated and killed. What little evidence there is for the manner of his death suggests that he fell at the head of his knights while leading a desperate all-or-nothing charge against the king. Hotspur displayed the virtues and defects of the knightly classes of his time; he was a bold fighting man rather than a subtle strategist or wily tactician, and in battle his nature was fiery and his instinct was to lead from the front.

Hotspur as military commander

There is no doubt, as the division of his force and the immediate launch of his left wing against the Scots' position show, that Hotspur devised a battle plan before he arrived at Otterburn. He has been criticized, not least by the author of the *Westminster Chronicle*, for attacking the Scots so rashly, so late in the day, and without 'drawing up his troops in battle formation'. This last omission was probably the main cause of his defeat and could have been avoided. The Scots capitalized on this mistake by attacking with their spearmen, under favourable conditions, before the English brought their archers into play, much as they had at Bannockburn, and with the same result. With the benefit of hindsight it seems obvious that he could have made victory almost certain by waiting for the morning, when he could have used the firepower of his archers to deadly effect. Yet the Scots would have realized this and most probably would have slipped away under cover of darkness, thus denying Hotspur the opportunity to salvage his dinted honour. Despite Hotspur's defeat both his popularity and his military reputation seem to have remained intact; the King granted him £1,000 towards his huge ransom and parliament contributed a further £3,000 in response to a petition of the 'knights of the counties and commonality of England'.

Sir Ralph Percy was Hotspur's younger brother; he was about 19 years old in 1388 and was embarking on a military career that ended with his death in 1400, when, according to R. White, he was 'slain by the saracens'.

Sir Mathew Redman, of Levens Hall in Westmorland, was the governor of Berwick-upon-Tweed; his troops, along with those of the Northumbrian knight Sir Robert Ogle, formed the left wing of Hotspur's army at Otterburn. Both these knights appear to have been professional soldiers who saw much service in defence of the Border.

Sir Thomas Umfraville, titular Earl of Angus and Lord of Redesdale, and his brother **Sir Robert Umfraville**, were prominent Northumbrian knights with long experience of border warfare. Robert later served under both Henry IV and his son, Henry V; he fought at Humbleton Hill in 1402 and served at sea against the Scots, becoming Vice-Admiral of England in 1410. He was made a Knight of the Garter, and fought at the siege of Harfleur, and at the battle of Agincourt in 1415. He died in 1436, the last of the Umfraville lords of Redesdale. The presence of the Umfravilles at Otterburn has been questioned. Only Hardyng, who should be reliable as he was at one time in the service of Sir Robert, gives them a part in the battle: as leaders of the left wing. Other sources omit mention of the Umfravilles and assign command of the English left wing to the less prominent knights: Sir Mathew Redman and Sir Robert Ogle.

He sent the lorde syr Thomas Umfeuyle,
His brother Robert, & also syr Thomas Grey,
And syr Mawe Redmayn beyond ye Scottes that whyle,
To hold them in that they fled not away;

Hardyng, Chronicle

The lord bishop of Durham was involved in civil and military affairs as well as ecclesiastical matters. John Fordham was prominent in political affairs and is shown on his palatinate seal accoutred as a knight, mounted and in full armour. In 1388 his baronial opponents succeeded in having him replaced as lord bishop by Walter Skirlaw, who proved to be an amiable and less turbulent incumbent of the see. This occurred by virtue of a papal bull of 3 April 1388. However his tenure of the see may only date from 1389. Opinion is divided as to which of these men appeared with his troops at Otterburn after the battle, though John Fordham has the best military credentials.

OPPOSING ARMIES

THE SCOTTISH ARMY

The troops mustered under the earl of Fife on the lower Jed Water in 1388 formed one of the strongest Scottish medieval armies ever to take the field. The call to arms echoed throughout the land, though the majority of men were drawn from the lowlands and from the populous north-east of the country. Contemporary sources make no mention of Highlanders within the army; however this cannot be taken as evidence that they were not present. Despite their numerical strength the Scots posed no real danger to the great border fortress of Carlisle as they did not have the siege equipment necessary to capture strongly fortified English towns and castles. Apart from widespread destruction, there was little to report at the time about the Scots' incursion into the West March, and consequently we have less knowledge of the main Scottish army than of the smaller force with which Douglas invaded the East March with such dramatic results.

Jean Froissart borrowed the following passage from the earlier writer Jean le Bel, who had first-hand knowledge of the Scots, having served in the Weardale campaign in 1327; he reveals the essence of late medieval Scottish armies:

> When they cross the border they advance sixty to seventy miles in a day and night, which would seem astonishing to anyone ignorant of their customs. The explanation is that, on their expeditions into England, they all come on horseback, except the irregulars who follow on foot. The knights and squires are mounted on fine, strong horses and the commoners on small ponies. Because they have to pass over the wild hills of Northumberland, they bring no baggage carts.

An astonishing rate of advance such as this could only have been kept up for a short time, after which the rate of progress must have slowed to a more sustainable pace. The Scots carried no wine or bread, preferring to drink from streams and eat the half-cooked flesh of plundered cattle, boiled in their own skins. They carried a little sack of oatmeal behind the saddle which, mixed with water to form a cake, they cooked on a large flat stone set on the fire. The horses were turned loose to graze untethered whenever the Scots dismounted; they needed fodder in great quantities, which generally restricted the operation of large mounted forces to the summer months when grazing was available.

The feudal levies that formed a large part of medieval Scottish armies were raised by 'Scottish Service', which was a levy of able-bodied freemen aged 16 to 60, who owed military service; they were to muster within eight days for 40 days' service and were organized into units of 5, 10, 100 and upwards, suggesting a sound command structure. These men were landholders of some substance who were expected to have armour and weapons, according to their means, as specified by government edicts. Scottish armies were not paid, yet service could be profitable, as invasions of England brought opportunities for robbery and the extortion of protection money and ransoms. Inspections, or *wapinshaws*, were held regularly, though the Scots do not seem to have been as well equipped as their English counterparts and a contemporary report of their turnout for the 1385 campaign describes them as 'all badly armed'. The French put in an appearance in Scotland in that year and provided subsidy and equipment to remedy deficiencies. By the later 14th century contracts or bonds of retinue, similar to English indentured contracts, were becoming widespread as a means of raising troops.

The strength of the Scottish invasion forces

Medieval chroniclers are unreliable regarding numbers and the otherwise reliable Westminster chronicler is no exception. For instance, he states that the Scots mustered 30,000 fighting men, and Froissart, who was no stranger to exaggeration, says that at Jedburgh, prior to the invasion, the combined forces of the Scots numbered 1,200 'spears' or mounted men, and fully 40,000 others. The latter huge figure is simply a device to emphasize his statement that 'There had not been seen for sixty years so numerous an assembly.' However, when smaller numbers are involved it is rather different and both Westminster and Froissart's figures can be taken seriously. This is the case when the latter says that the earl of Douglas' force consisted of 'three or four hundred spears', and in a later passage, 'three hundred picked lances', in other words, men-at-arms, and 'two thousand stout infantry and archers, all well mounted'. The ratio of mounted men-at-arms to infantry in these figures is plausible too as this was about one to seven at this time. If we examine Froissart's figures for the muster at Jedburgh we must disregard his figure of 40,000 infantry as clearly exaggerated. We may however place some reliance on his smaller figure of 1,200 for the number of mounted men-at-arms, which if multiplied by seven gives a more realistic total of 8,400 for the foot; this gives a total strength of 9,600 men for the main Scottish army. If we multiply Douglas' 300 men-at-arms by seven this gives us 2,100 infantry, or rather mounted infantry, and allows Douglas a total force of 2,400 men. This would make the earl of Fife's force four times stronger than that of Douglas, which is believable and may be the truth. It is unlikely, however, that all those included in these totals would be effective fighting men; the numbers could be taken to include a proportion of servants and boys to hold the horses and,

A Scottish spearman, typical of those who formed the bulk of the armies that fought at Otterburn and Humbleton Hill. His body defence consists of a jack or *akheton*, which was a form of soft armour that was stuffed with layers of linen, wool or even twisted straw, then quilted to preserve its shape, and which proved effective against sword cuts and arrows. An early 14th-century statute, intended to rectify the poor turnout of Scottish armies, laid down that a man worth £10 of moveable property should be equipped with an akheton, bascinet, gauntlets, sword and spear. Scottish spears were 12–14ft long at the time of Otterburn; later their length was extended up to 18ft 6in. (Author's illustration)

particularly in the case of the main army on the West March, a good many camp followers.

Knights and men-at-arms

Scotland, being a poor country with a relatively small population, did not have the resources to field a heavy cavalry force to match that of her powerful southern neighbour. Scottish knights and men-at-arms were armed in much the same manner as their English counterparts; there is some evidence that arms and armour were manufactured in Scotland in the 14th century and, though national styles were slow to evolve, swords of particularly Scottish style can be readily identified. It was not unusual for Scots to have served in foreign armies; Sir John Swinton, for example, had fought alongside the duke of Lancaster in France and must have had a sound knowledge of English tactics. Though there were mounted archers with the Scottish army during the Otterburn campaign, the role of the mounted infantry was to fight on foot, in the manner of the men-at-arms. They were simply less well equipped and of lower social status than the knights and men-at-arms to whom Froissart refers as 'picked lances'. Distinctions of rank and status in society were blurred at Otterburn, where all the combatants dismounted and fought on foot; the mounted infantry took their place in the line of battle alongside the more heavily armoured men-at-arms, while the knights provided the officers for the units of men-at-arms and added a stiffening to the fighting line.

Scottish archers

Scottish archers were drawn from the Borders and southern Scotland, and those of Selkirk Forest were justly famed for their prowess with the longbow. They did not, however, match the English archers in numbers, nor were they employed with the same tactical skill in battle; nevertheless, by the 15th century they were being recruited by the French in large numbers, in an attempt to counter the dominance of the English longbowmen. Highlanders, from the wild West Highlands, are known to have used the bow, though we have no evidence that they were present in the army of 1388 in significant numbers.

Scottish tactics

The Scots were not strong in archers and lacked a heavy cavalry arm; consequently they relied heavily on their spearmen who, though they rode to battle, fought on foot in manoeuvrable though densely packed formations, several ranks deep. They looked back to the time when Robert Bruce's schiltrons of spearmen had defeated the English at Bannockburn without realizing that it was the disorganization of the enemy and their inability to co-ordinate infantry with cavalry, or use their archers effectively, that had contributed to Bruce's victory as much as his skill in employing his spearmen. After Bruce's time conditions changed; English tactics evolved and the longbowman, to whom the Scots had no answer, ruled the battlefield. This was amply demonstrated by disastrous defeats at Dupplin Muir, Hallidon Hill and Neville's Cross, which caused the Scottish

Grave slab of Gilbert of Grenlaw, killed at the battle of Harlaw in 1411; Kinkell, Aberdeenshire. Gilbert's monument shows the style of armour in use in Scotland in the early 15th century. His sword is of distinctive Scottish pattern, though the rest of his equipment is similar in style to that of his English counterparts, exemplified by the Felbrigge brass. Though none has survived, we know that armour was produced in Scotland in medieval times, for there exists a writ issued in 1400 by the Chancellor to the Mayor of London, who had arrested the 'harnoises made by John of Wardelawe of Scotland for the Earl of March viz 5 bacynettes, 4 pr, of plates with 5 brestplatez 6 braciers, 6 garnicements pour lances, gauntez de fer, 2 escuez, 6 selles bastardes'. (Author's illustration)

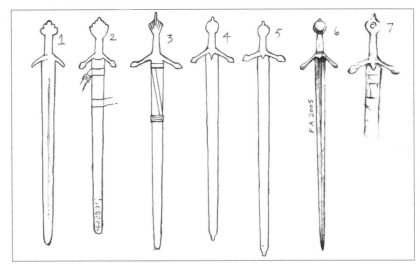

Sir Alexander Ramsay of Dalhousie was a knight of Midlothian and an adherent of the earl of Douglas. He fought at the battle of Otterburn and at the combat of Nisbet Muir in 1402; he was killed at Humbleton Hill in September of the same year. Sir Alexander holds his crested helm, an item that had been relegated to tournament use by the 1380s, and was not worn in battle. The articulated plates of his body armour are held together by being riveted to an outer covering, which is faced with decorative velvet. Sir Alexander's armour is of Italian manufacture and is based on surviving artefacts. (Author's illustration)

ABOVE, RIGHT Scottish medieval swords. (1–5) Swords from medieval West Highland monuments. (6) Sword of about 1400, with typical depressed quillions and disc pommel, similar to that shown on the seal of John Balliol (above). (7) Similar sword to fig. (6), from the monument of Gilbert Grenlaw. (Author's illustration)

leadership to be wary of open battle and to accept that, in the long run, Fabian tactics might be more effective in pursuing their aims.

THE ENGLISH ARMY

English strategy in defence of the Border against Scottish incursions relied increasingly on fortification and this is reflected by the programme of castle building in the northern counties in the late 14th century. The troops permanently stationed on the Border were supplemented by levied troops from the northern counties in times of danger. The main Scottish Border strongholds, such as Roxburgh and Lochmaben, remained in English hands throughout much of this time, though Lochmaben became increasingly untenable and was recaptured in 1384. The Scottish response to English invasion was invariably a Fabian strategy, combining withdrawal with a scorched earth policy, to deny any source of succour to the enemy.

Levying troops for the defence of the border

The defence of the Border was in the care of the wardens of the Marches; the office of warden and the manner in which the affairs of the Marches were regulated were in place by the 1340s. There were three Scottish Marches, East, Middle and West, but only two English ones as there was no Middle March at this time. The wardens had a certain number of regular troops under their command; for example, in March 1389 Thomas Mowbray, Earl of Nottingham, contracted with the Crown to keep the East March and to retain a force of 400 men-at-arms and 800 archers during the dangerous months of June and July. Hotspur's contract, as warden of the East March in 1388, must have provided him with a similar force and it is probable that these troops formed the nucleus of the army that the Percys assembled in Newcastle before Otterburn. Generally, troops raised in the northern counties formed the armies employed against the Scots, and this is true of the Otterburn campaign, in which all the knights we know to have taken part were northerners.

There were levies from the town of Newcastle itself, raised, if not commanded, by the sheriff, Sir Ralph Eure. Sir Mathew Redman, as governor of Berwick, would have brought troops from his garrison there, and the presence in Newcastle of the seneschal of York suggests a contribution of men from that city too.

The troops serving in Hotspur's personal retinue, those from the garrison of Berwick, and many other contingents would have been raised by indentured contract in the same manner as the men who formed the backbone of the English armies that served in France. By the 1380s feudal levies were increasingly rare in overseas armies; nevertheless, a proportion of troops would still have been raised for short-term service in England by being impressed by commission of array. Under this system commissioners, usually knights, or members of the king's household, were called upon by the Crown to select quotas of men from both shires and towns, selecting 'the strongest and most vigorous' of those with an obligation to military service. An inspection of those eligible for service and their equipment was held twice a year, which was supposed to ensure the efficiency of these levies. They were organized into units of 20 men commanded by *vintenars*, which in turn were organized into larger formations of 100 under a *centenar*; larger units of a thousand men were led by an officer known as a *millenar*. Once outside their county or town boundary these levies were paid by the king and were expected to serve for 40 days. The system made considerable manpower available; for example, the county of Yorkshire alone put over 3,000 mounted archers in the field before the battle of Neville's Cross in 1346. The border county levies were expected to form a first line of defence against the Scots and were supplemented in time of war by troops raised generally in the more northerly counties. Though potentially there was no shortage of manpower in 1388, the quality of these levied troops was at best uneven. The bishop of Durham's force was probably largely composed of levies and Hotspur did not wait to be reinforced by these but pursued the retreating Scots with the troops he had to hand.

Sir Henry Percy, called Hotspur, in full panoply of arms. Hotspur's helm displays his crest, a lion azure with a label gules. (Model by the author)

Strength of the English army at Otterburn

As noted above, medieval chroniclers are notoriously unreliable when reporting the numerical strength of armies. Their exaggerated numbers often seem ridiculous, though really these inflated numbers are simply their way of saying 'a great many'. However, when reporting smaller numbers they are often far more realistic and their estimates can be considered seriously. Froissart tells us that 'six hundred spears of knights and squires and upwards of eight thousand infantry' set out from Newcastle to march to Otterburn, '… more than enough to fight the Scots, who were but three hundred lances and two thousand others.' In this case, Froissart's smaller number of 600 for the mounted men-at-arms seems plausible. The larger number of 8,000 infantry seems rather high and needs to be considered. In the 1380s, the usual proportion of men-at-arms to infantry was about one to seven. If we take 600 men-at-arms to be correct, and multiply this by seven, we arrive at a lower, more realistic figure of 4,200 infantry. This would allow Hotspur a total of 4,800 men; still more than enough to fight the Scots whom, by this reckoning, he would out-number by slightly more than two to one, which is a more credible state of affairs than Froissart's 'three to one'.

However, the battlefield of Otterburn lies fully 31 miles from Newcastle, twice the distance that a medieval army would have covered in a normal day's march. It seems probable, on this account, that Hotspur's force consisted entirely of mounted men, both archers and armoured men-at-arms, which argues for a smaller rather than a larger force. It is unlikely that Hotspur had 4,200 mounted troops on hand in Newcastle, and suspect that the English army would have, at best, out-numbered the Scots only slightly.

Both Walter Bower, in his *Scotichronicon*, and the author of the *Orygynale Cronykil* give Douglas' strength as nearly 7,000 men, and that of Hotspur as 10,000. These may be inflated numbers, but the relative strength of the armies is credible; these are sober, considered figures that, being from Scottish sources, might have been expected to exaggerate the numerical superiority of the English. The truth of the matter seems to be that the armies at Otterburn were more evenly matched than Froissart would have us believe.

Mounted archers

The realization that the highly mobile Scots needed to be caught before they could be brought to battle, and that the English heavy cavalry were not the instrument to achieve this, led to the development of mounted infantry. Evidence from surviving indentured contracts demonstrates that the mounted archer was replacing, though not entirely, those on foot as the 14th century wore on. An early record of mounted archers occurs in 1337, when the army mustered at Newcastle by the earl of Salisbury consisted of 60 knights, 450 men-at-arms, 466 Welsh foot and 1,970 horse archers, a very high proportion of mounted archers for this time, no doubt prompted by the particular requirements of Scottish service. Early sources often refer to 'each man-at-arms and his archer', indicating an equal proportion of archers to men-at-arms, though by the later years of Edward III the ratio had increased to two to one. The earl of Nottingham, for example, contracted in 1389 to keep the East March and Berwick-upon-Tweed for a year at a cost of £2,000 per annum, retaining a force of 400 men-at-arms and 800 archers during the dangerous months of June and July. By the early 15th century the ratio was even higher: frequently five or even six archers to each man-at-arms. A number of packhorses, to carry equipment as well as sheaves of arrows, would have been allocated to each unit of mounted archers and further swelled the already large amount of horseflesh needed to transport an army in the field.

Horse archers were armed with the longbow; they dismounted to fight and a number of men must have been told to watch the horses as the fighting force formed into hollow wedges, in the same manner as their foot comrades. Their mounts were simply a means of transportation, and their value reflects this; in 1346 the average archer's nag was

A well-armed English mounted archer of the household of the earl of Northumberland. His armour consists of a padded and quilted *jack*, over which is worn a sleeveless surcoat, on which is displayed the silver crescent badge of the Percys. His bascinet has no visor, though there is an attached mail aventail (movable front or mouthpiece of the helmet); plate gauntlets protect the hands. At his hip hang a sword and a buckler – a small one-handed shield in use in the swordplay of the time. The longbow is illustrated without a handle or horn knocks – medieval illustrations never show longbows with handles, though horn knocks are sometimes depicted. Arrows were supplied in sheaves, bundled in cloth drawstring bags, which were sometimes used as a sort of quiver; otherwise arrows were simply stuck through the belt; the over-the-shoulder style, or 'Robin Hood' quiver, was not used in a military context. (Author's illustration)

The monumental brass of Sir William Echingham of 1387, in Etchingham Church, Sussex, provides contemporary evidence of the style of armour of the best-equipped men-at-arms and knights at Otterburn. Plate armour by this time had been devised to protect most parts of the body though a padded mail aventail, fastened to the bascinet, was used to allow articulation of the head. The visor is omitted on practically all monumental brasses in order to show the face, which in the odd case may be a portrait. The armour is simple in style with minimal decoration and designed with function rather than display in mind. (Author's illustration)

worth only £1; in comparison, a man-at-arms' charger, a real cavalry mount, was valued around £10. Household archers, such as those retained by contract by Hotspur and his father, may have been better mounted than the levies and probably served in a variety of roles, providing scouts and messengers for the army. Pay reflected status and in the 1380s the mounted archer received 6d a day, the same rate as the lower ranks of the men-at-arms, though double the pay of lowly foot archers who had only 3d. The Neville's Cross campaign of 1346 demonstrates the large proportion of mounted archers raised to combat a Scottish invasion force. Lancashire's contribution to the campaign was a contingent of four knights, 60 men-at-arms, 240 foot archers and 960 horse archers. Yorkshire's contingent of archers appears to have been entirely mounted, fully 3,020 of them, along with a paltry 15 men-at-arms and, surprisingly, a small number of *hobelars*, a type of light cavalryman who by this time had all but been supplanted in English armies by the mounted archer. The horse archer did not replace the foot archer altogether; they remained in existence alongside their mounted comrades and must have been formed in quite separate units and marched at their own pace.

Medieval armies generally marched about 15 miles a day, which we can take to be the pace of the troops on foot, and of the carts and wagons of the baggage train. Large bodies of mounted troops, operating without the constraints of infantry and wheeled transport, moved more rapidly; though it is difficult to be specific, there is no reason why the English, similarly mounted to the Scots, could not match their rate of progress (see the beginning of this chapter). The 31-mile stretch between Newcastle and Otterburn was twice the distance that the infantry would be expected to achieve in a day but was, as events prove, attainable for mounted troops.

English men-at-arms

Hotspur's army consisted of two types of troops only: those who fought in the role of men-at-arms (comprising knights, esquires, men-at-arms and spearmen), and the archers who supported them. Although the men-at-arms were cavalrymen, and were armed and mounted accordingly, they increasingly fulfilled the role of armoured infantry in battle, fighting dismounted alongside the archers in a solid formation bristling with spears, in much the same manner as the Scottish spearmen formed up in their schiltrons. There were a variety of ranks among the men-at-arms; the lower ranks were divided between esquires, whose social status might allow them to aspire to knighthood, and *armati*, or men-at-arms drawn from the common or non-gentle classes. The knights, who officered the army, were either high-ranking bannerets, or ordinary knights, sometimes known as knights bachelor, who ranked below them. Degrees of rank were reflected both by the quality of their mounts and by their wages; a banneret had 4s a day, a knight 2s, an esquire 1s, and an *armati* 6d, the same as a mounted archer. There were usually at least 12 men-at-arms to each knight. It is possible to identify about 40 English knights and esquires who fought at Otterburn; most of these were from the counties of Northumberland, Durham, Cumberland, Westmorland and Yorkshire. In addition, there were several Gascon esquires at Otterburn who fought in the service of the Percys; two of them met Froissart at Orthez in 1389 and are named by him as his informants on the details of the battle.

English tactics

At Falkirk, in 1298, the English heavy cavalry had proved a blunt and ineffective weapon against the bristling schiltrons of steady Scottish pikemen. Only after Edward I's bowmen came up and unleashed an arrow storm into the faces of the immobile ranks of spearmen were the mounted men-at-arms able to bludgeon their way into the resultant great rents in the ranks of the schiltrons, and finish the job. Edward II, unlike his father, was no soldier; at Bannockburn in 1314, the arrogant and ill-disciplined knighthood of England, acting independently, and scorning all co-ordination with their infantry, were destroyed by the spearmen of Scotland's great warrior king, Robert Bruce. Edward seems to have learned nothing from his humiliation at Bannockburn; years after his defeat he still imagined that armoured spearmen on foot were the answer to Scottish tactics. After Bannockburn, in King Robert's time, the Scots had the upper hand militarily; but it did not last, and his death marked the end of their ascendancy. In 1322, at Boroughbridge, Andrew de Harcla dismounted his men-at-arms and formed them up in a schiltron, in what at the time was considered 'the Scottish fashion'. The men-at-arms were flanked by strong bodies of archers with the river Ure and its bridge between them and the forces of the rebel earls. Their attack made no impression on Harcla's dispositions and the rebel army lost heart and dispersed, leaving the earls prisoners of the royal army. Boroughbridge was an early demonstration of the tactics that were soon to become the English fashion of fighting. Yet the lesson of Boroughbridge was not learned immediately; during the disastrous campaign in Weardale in 1327, the English still relied on heavy cavalry as their main weapon against the more lightly armed and nimble Scots, who were able to evade their attempts to bring them to battle with impunity.

Shortly after Edward III took the throne of England in 1327, there occurred a revolution in English tactics that overthrew the Scottish military ascendancy and made possible Edward and the Black Prince's continental victories. On Dupplin Muir, in 1332, the Scots had due warning, when Edward Balliol and Henry de Beaumont's small though well-organized band of self-seeking adventurers defeated a large but unwieldy Scottish army composed mainly of levied spearmen. Beaumont was a professional soldier, and it may have been a mixture of his experience and sheer practical necessity that led to his massing his archers on the flanks of the dismounted men-at-arms in a strong position, forcing the Scots to make a frontal attack into a hail of arrows. The resultant debacle was so one-sided that the Scots should have been warned. But the lesson was not learned, and at Hallidon Hill, the following year, they came on in the same old way, and were even more heavily defeated. Edward III's army adopted a more fully developed formation than that employed by Beaumont at Dupplin, which allowed the archers to slaughter the advancing Scottish spearmen long before they could close with the English men-at-arms. The Scots had no answer; the tables had turned with a vengeance.

By the 1380s English tactics were well established; strong formations of men-at-arms were flanked by equal numbers of archers, with a mounted cavalry reserve; when posted in a favourable position this proved a formidable combination. Neither the archers nor the men-at-arms were battle winners on their own; the two arms were complementary, and only when employed in combination with the

Monumental brass of Sir George Felbrigge who died in 1400, in Playford Church, Suffolk. Sir George's brass displays the armour of the early 15th century and is typical of that of the knights who fought at Humbleton Hill. The workmanship of the Playford brass is of a higher order than that at Etchingham, and far more detail of the construction of the armour and of its decoration is included. The two brasses have many similarities, though the armour of the Playford knight is far richer in decoration and displays some evolution of construction, particularly in the case of the poleyns, or knee defences. Sir George's sword has an unusually long hilt and may be a representation of a hand and a half sword. The lion on the heraldic jupon would have been inlayed in red at one time. (Author's illustration)

other was their effectiveness maximized. As English armies increasingly fielded large bodies of mounted archers to support their men-at-arms, the Scots' advantage in mobility became a thing of the past. The value of horse archers lay in their ability to muster quickly and move rapidly to bring the Scots to action. The victories of Neville's Cross and Humbleton Hill testify eloquently to their effectiveness.

Hotspur had experience enough to be aware of the tactical realities of his day and, though his mounted force allowed him a rapidity of movement that enabled him to surprise the Scots at Otterburn, his impetuous advance ignored sound tactical principles and the resulting disorganization brought him to disaster.

ORDERS OF BATTLE

THE BATTLE OF OTTERBURN, 5 AUGUST 1388

THE SCOTTISH ARMY
Commander-in-Chief James, second Earl of Douglas

The left wing
Commanded by the earl of Douglas
200 knights, esquires and men-at-arms
1,200 spearmen and archers, dismounted

The right wing
Commanded by the earl of March and the earl of Moray
100 knights, esquires and men-at-arms
900 spearmen and archers, dismounted

The servants
500 lightly armed irregulars and youths

THE ENGLISH ARMY
Commander-in-Chief Sir Henry Percy, called 'Hotspur'

The right wing
Commanded by Sir Henry Percy and his brother Sir Ralph Percy
300 dismounted knights, esquires and men-at-arms
2,100 mounted infantry, archers and spearmen, dismounted

The left wing
Commanded by Sir Mathew Redman and Sir Robert Ogle
100 knights, esquires and men-at-arms
700 mounted infantry, archers and spearmen, dismounted

Due to the contradictory nature of the sources these numbers are the author's estimate.

OPPOSING PLANS

SCOTTISH PLANS

The invasions of 1388 were intended to cause destruction in the English northern counties on a scale that would force the English government to concede the argument over Scottish independence in exchange for peace. It has even been suggested that the Scots planned to capture Carlisle, and to hold the city as a bargaining counter in future negotiations. Earlier in the 14th century, Robert Bruce had employed a similar course of action with success, though the political crisis in England at that time had favoured his strategy, which might not have succeeded under normal circumstances. It was a short-lived success anyway, a fact that the Scottish leadership of the 1380s may have chosen to ignore when they pursued a similar aggressive policy. In 1388, political convulsions in England distracted Richard II from Scottish affairs and encouraged the Scots in their warlike plans. However, the baronial party, or Lords Appellant, who temporarily usurped Richard's power, were themselves a war party; they were opposed to peace with France, and would be unlikely to make any concessions to Scottish aggression. The ordinary Scots, who made up the armies of Fife and Douglas, were probably unconcerned with such matters, being preoccupied with the business of plundering the livestock and goods of their southern neighbours, and with the profit to be gained from the ransom of rich captives.

The castle at Carlingford in Ireland was described as 'out of repair and unsafe' in 1388 when the Scots burnt the town. They 'plundered the castle, and loaded 15 Irish ships which lay at anchor in the harbour with all the goods taken from the town. Marvellously enriched with these, they set out for home with a large fleet. On their way back they plundered the Isle of Man ... at the port of Loch Ryan in Galloway, they landed well satisfied.' *Scotichronicon* (Photo, Colin McKay)

Early in 1388, a Scottish force attacked and burnt Carlingford in Ireland, then raided the Isle of Man, before returning home laden with plunder. It is possible that this raid was launched as part of a Scottish master plan that aimed to damage the English on a wide front in 1388. The earl of Fife's invasion of the West March of England was the pivotal event on which the plans turned. The earl of Douglas' simultaneous diversionary attack was aimed to confuse as well as damage the enemy in the East March. Yet Walter Bower's suggestion that Douglas' raid into the East March was not part of Fife's original plan calls the existence of a Scottish master plan into question and evokes an alternative proposition: that Scottish military operations in 1388 were not governed by a co-ordinated plan at all, and that both the Irish affair and Douglas' raid were simply the results of individual opportunism.

ENGLISH PLANS

The wardens of the Marches had troops available in garrison to counter the Scottish threat, and levies from further south could be summoned when the situation demanded reinforcements. In 1388 there seems to have been no organized resistance to the Scottish invasion of the West March. In the East March, of which we have more information, though the Scots marauded unmolested in the countryside, they did not seriously threaten the strongly garrisoned castles. Newcastle itself was packed with troops under Hotspur, awaiting an opportunity to respond to the Scottish invasion, and the bishop of Durham was bringing up reinforcements from further south. Clearly the Percys planned an aggressive response to the invasion and, though instructions from the government may have led Hotspur to remain behind his fortifications during the first days of Douglas' incursion, when the situation became clear Hotspur did not lose the opportunity of bringing the Scots to battle.

These carved Irish warriors of the late 14th century display a marked similarity to those found on West Highland monuments of the same period; 'eight hundred armed horsemen' from Dundalk came to the assistance of the men of Carlingford, but according to the *Scotichronicon* the 200 Scots raiders had the better of them all. (Photos, Colin McKay)

English plans, in response to a Scottish invasion, included a riposte or counter-invasion, as Froissart's dialogue explains:

> if the Scots enter the country through Cumberland by Carlisle, we will ride into Scotland and do them more damage than they can do to us; for theirs is an open country, which may be entered anywhere, but ours is the contrary, with strong and well fortified towns and castles.

It was calculated that an English army creating havoc in Scotland would cause widespread alarm and demoralization among the Scots who had left their homes and families unprotected and at the mercy of the English, and that this might lead to widespread desertion and an early termination of the invasion. It was a plan that the earl of Northumberland was well placed at Alnwick to carry out in response to Fife's invasion in the West March; however, Douglas' raid into the East March confused matters and led to the abandonment of this course of action.

THE CAMPAIGN OF 1388

THE SCOTS MUSTER IN THE FOREST OF JEDBURGH

Yt fell abowght the Lamasse tyde
When husbondes wynne ther haye,
The dowghtye Dowglasse bowynd him to ryde
In Ynglond to take a praye.

Reliques of Ancient English Poetry

Froissart's version of the events of the fateful year of Otterburn begins with a feast held at Aberdeen, attended by the Scottish lords, where it was decided 'that in the middle of August of the year 1388, they would assemble all their forces at a castle called Jedworth, situated ... on the borders of Cumberland'. The king, according to the chronicler, was not informed of their intentions. At this time, Robert II, King of Scots, was 71 years of age and approaching the end of his reign. Due to his age and infirmity, his eldest son and heir, John, Earl of Carrick, had taken over the reins of government from his father as Guardian of the kingdom in 1384. Although a kick from a horse had left him disabled and unable to take the field in person, Carrick and his supporters, among whom the earl of Douglas was prominent, were clearly instigators of the policy that led to war. There is no evidence to support Froissart's tale of the meeting in Aberdeen; nevertheless, the Scots leadership did gather their forces in late summer in the forest of Jedburgh near Southdean Church, in the valley of the upper Jed Water, about four miles north of the frontier at the Redeswire. The castle of Jedburgh was still at this time in the hands of the English and would remain so until 1409 when it was taken and slighted by the 'mediocres', or ordinary folk, of Teviotdale.

Strategically the assembly place was well chosen, for it threatened both the East and West Marches of England, so that the direction of the attack would not be known until it was launched. The muster was on a scale not seen for many years, and was most probably the result of a full-scale general call-up throughout Scotland. When intelligence of the massing of Scottish troops behind the Cheviots was brought to the Percys by their network of informants, they realized the seriousness of the situation and despatched messengers to alert the northern counties to the threat and to warn them to put their defences in order.

The Scots, according to Froissart, got wind of English plans for a counter-invasion of Scotland when they captured a talkative spy, who had been sent by the earl of Northumberland to discover their strength and intentions. In response to his tale the Scots' leaders devised a diversionary raid, to be led by the earl of Douglas, into the East March. This was intended as a means of preventing an English counter-invasion

SCOTTISH INVASIONS

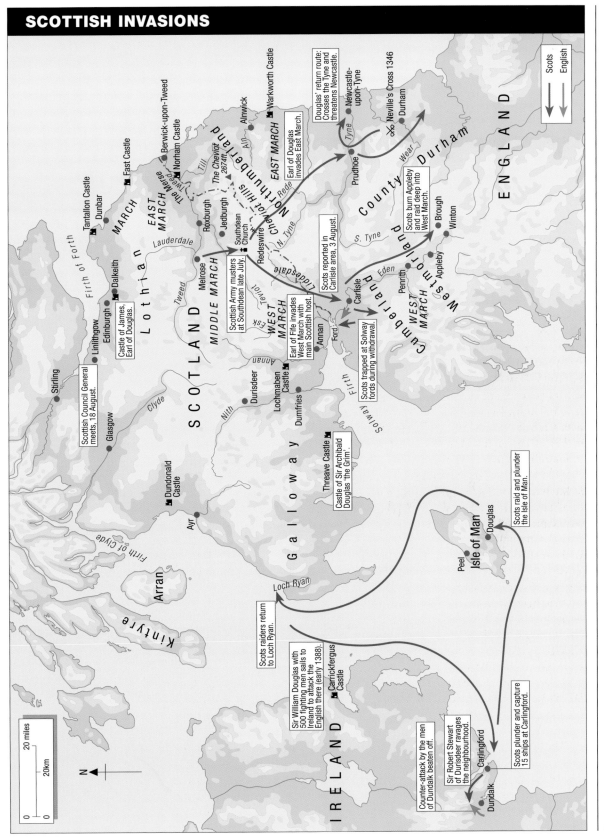

Scots
English

Warkworth Castle

Alnwick

EAST MARCH

Earl of Douglas
invades East March.

Douglas' return route:
Crosses the Tyne and
threatens Newcastle.

Newcastle-
upon-Tyne

Neville's Cross 1346

Durham

County Durham

ENGLAND

Prudhoe

Scots burn Appleby
and raid deep into
West March.

Brough

Winton

Berwick-upon-Tweed

Norham Castle

The Cheviot
2674ft.

Scots reported in
Carlisle area, 3 August.

S. Tyne

East Castle

Dunbar

Tantallon Castle

Roxburgh

Jedburgh

Southdean
Church

Redeswire

Scottish Army musters
at Southdean late July.

Carlisle

Appleby

Penrith

Eden

West March

Westmorland

Cumberland

Firth of Forth

Lauderdale

MIDDLE MARCH

Melrose

WEST MARCH

Earl of Fife invades
West March with
main Scottish host.

Ford

Scots trapped at Solway
fords during withdrawal.

Edinburgh

Linlithgow

Dalkeith

Lothian

Castle of James,
Earl of Douglas.

Tweed

Annan

Durisdeer

Stirling

Glasgow

Scottish Council General
meets, 18 August.

Clyde

Nith

Lochmaben
Castle

Dumfries

Solway Firth

Dundonald
Castle

Ayr

Galloway

Threave Castle

Castle of Sir Archibald
Douglas 'the Grim'.

Arran

Firth of Clyde

Kintyre

Loch Ryan

Scots raiders return
to Loch Ryan.

Scots raid and plunder
the Isle of Man.

Isle of Man

Peel

Douglas

Sir William Douglas
with 500 fighting men sails to
Ireland to attack the
English there (early 1388).

Carrickfergus
Castle

IRELAND

Counter-attack by the men
of Dundalk beaten off.

Sir Robert Stewart
of Durisdeer ravages
the neighbourhood.

Carlingford

Scots plunder and capture
15 ships at Carlingford.

Dundalk

20 miles

20km

N

35

Hermitage Castle, 'The strength of Liddesdale', had been a Douglas possession since 1371 and its present appearance owes much to their rebuilding work. The earl of Fife and his army passed this way in August 1388, on their way to Carlisle. (Author's photo)

and of spreading confusion, which would delay enemy reaction until it was too late, allowing the raiders time to re-cross the frontier. Scottish sources suggest another version of events, this being that Douglas had agreed to accompany the earl of Fife's army but went back on this arrangement and led his own following into the East March instead. Whatever the truth of the matter, Douglas' raid was a brilliant success, though, as we shall see, he did not re-cross the Border, but stopped short at Otterburn, with dramatic consequences.

THE EARL OF FIFE INVADES THE WEST MARCH

The invasion of England may have been set to start on 1 August, certainly no later; the best we can say is that about this time the earl of Fife and Sir Archibald Douglas 'the Grim', with the main Scottish host, left Southdean and crossed the Cheviots by way of the old track called the Wheel Causeway, into the head of Liddesdale, on their march to Carlisle. The itinerary of Edward I in 1298 suggests that the route from Jedburgh to Carlisle ran, in medieval times, past Wheel Church and followed the Wheel Causeway, which took the most direct route into Liddesdale. The route over Teviothead into Ewesdale, followed by the modern main road, would have entailed an extra day's march. The rate of progress of the average medieval army, including infantry, was no more than 15 miles a day, which would have made Carlisle a three-day march from Southdean. However there is little doubt that the majority of Fife's troops, at least the real fighting core of his army, were mounted men, who could be expected to reach Carlisle within two days. Their presence in the Carlisle area is documented by an English report as early as 3 August. By the 13th, Richard II was aware of the invasion, as he wrote indignantly to John of

The West Walls are an imposing remnant of the medieval walls of Carlisle, which were more than a match for the Scots in 1388. Without siege engines, they were unable to make any impression on the defences of the border city, though a great deal of damage was caused in the surrounding area. (Author's photo)

Gaunt in Gascony, asking for assistance and announcing his intention to set out against the Scots in person before the end of that month.

Two formidable warriors and their retinues, newly returned from a successful attack on English-held Ireland and a raid on the Isle of Man, augmented the army of the earl of Fife in the West March. These were Archibald the Grim's natural son, Sir William Douglas of Nithsdale, and Sir Robert Stewart of Durisdeer, both implacable foes of the English. In Cumberland, the passage of the Scots was marked by destruction, which was recorded at West Linton and Irthington, north of Carlisle, and at Burgh-by-Sands on the Solway and Sebergham to the west of Inglewood Forest, suggesting that the Scottish depredations were widespread. The raiders ranged on a broad front down the Eden Valley into Westmorland; Appleby was burned to the ground and damage was recorded at Brough and as far south as Winton, near Kirkby Stephen. On their return the Scots blockaded Carlisle for a time, but, as they had no siege engines, they could make no impression on the formidable defences of the town. Instead, they vented their frustration on the surrounding countryside, which was ravaged mercilessly, rendering the royal demesnes there quite valueless. When reports of the death of the earl of Douglas at Otterburn reached the Scottish leaders in the West March, they withdrew from England, taking with them, as well as their plunder, some 300 captives to hold for ransom, including Peter de Tilliol, the sheriff of Cumberland.

THE EARL OF DOUGLAS INVADES THE EAST MARCH

The earls of Fife and Douglas probably launched their separate invasions of England simultaneously, possibly as early as 28 July, but no later than 1 August. Walter Bower begins his account of the Otterburn campaign by relating the tale of Douglas going back on his undertaking

to accompany Fife into the West March and assembling his own following to invade the East March instead. This not only suggests division and tensions within the Scottish leadership, but also calls into question whether there was a co-ordinated master plan at all. The campaign may have been a purely haphazard affair. Whatever the truth of the matter, around 1 August, the earl of Douglas crossed the Redeswire into England; with him rode George Dunbar, Earl of March, and his younger brother, John Dunbar, Earl of Moray, together with an array of knights of Douglas' affinity, mostly drawn from the Lothians and Borders, each accompanied by a numerous following of men-at-arms, mounted spearmen and archers. Douglas' force advanced rapidly down Redesdale, unencumbered by infantry or baggage carts; such supplies as were deemed necessary being carried by packhorses.

> Over Ottercap hyll they came in,
> And so down by Rodelyffe cragge,
> Upon Grene Leyton they lyghted dowyn,
> Styrande many a stagge: [Mounted on many a horse]
> *Reliques of Ancient English Poetry*

The old ballads belong in the realm of folklore and tradition rather than history, yet the lines above are so striking that they are difficult to ignore and may preserve some memory of the Scots' route through Northumberland. If, for once, they are given credence, they indicate that the earl of Douglas, after crossing into England at the Redeswire, and riding down Redesdale past Otterburn, then moved in an easterly direction across the Ottercops Moss, by way of the old

The Redeswire is the border crossing, high in the Cheviot Hills, at the head of Redesdale, from where the road leads by way of the valley of the Carter Burn to Southdean on the lower Jed Water in Roxburghshire. The earl of Douglas followed this route into England, late in July 1388. (Author's photo)

38

THE EARL OF DOUGLAS INVADES

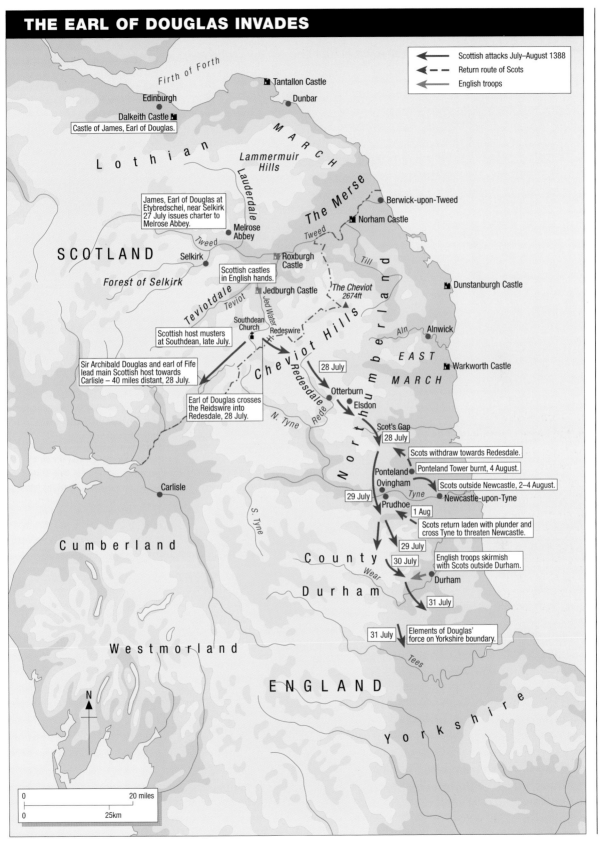

Legend:
- Scottish attacks July–August 1388
- Return route of Scots
- English troops

Firth of Forth

Tantallon Castle

Edinburgh
Dunbar

Dalkeith Castle
Castle of James, Earl of Douglas.

L o t h i a n

M A R C H

Lammermuir Hills

Berwick-upon-Tweed

Lauderdale

The Merse

Norham Castle

James, Earl of Douglas at Etybredschel, near Selkirk 27 July issues charter to Melrose Abbey.

Melrose Abbey

Tweed

Tweed

S C O T L A N D

Selkirk

Till

Roxburgh Castle

Dunstanburgh Castle

Forest of Selkirk

Scottish castles in English hands.

The Cheviot 2674ft

Teviotdale

Jedburgh Castle

Teviot

Jed Water

C h e v i o t   H i l l s

N o r t h u m b e r l a n d

Aln

Alnwick

Southdean Church

Redeswire

E A S T

Scottish host musters at Southdean, late July.

28 July

Redesdale

M A R C H

Warkworth Castle

Sir Archibald Douglas and earl of Fife lead main Scottish host towards Carlisle – 40 miles distant, 28 July.

Rede

Otterburn

Elsdon

Earl of Douglas crosses the Reidswire into Redesdale, 28 July.

N. Tyne

Scot's Gap

28 July

Scots withdraw towards Redesdale.

Ponteland

Ponteland Tower burnt, 4 August.

C u m b e r l a n d

Carlisle

S. Tyne

29 July

Ovingham

Tyne

Scots outside Newcastle, 2–4 August.

Newcastle-upon-Tyne

Prudhoe

1 Aug

Scots return laden with plunder and cross Tyne to threaten Newcastle.

29 July

C o u n t y

30 July

English troops skirmish with Scots outside Durham.

W e s t m o r l a n d

Wear

Durham

D u r h a m

31 July

31 July

Elements of Douglas' force on Yorkshire boundary.

E N G L A N D

N

Tees

Y o r k s h i r e

0   20 miles
0   25km

'Over Ottercap hyll they came in': *Reliques of Ancient English Poetry.* The dramatic landscape of the Cheviots unfolds northwards in this view from the evocatively named 'Winter's Gibbet', high on Ottercops Hill. The earl of Douglas might have paused here on his return before descending into Redesdale. (Author's photo)

'And so down to Rodelyffe cragge': *Reliques of Ancient English Poetry.* The rocky landmark of Rothley Crags would have marked the way south through Northumberland for Douglas and his army. View looking west towards Ottercops Hill. (Author's photo)

The eminence of Rothley Crags would have provided the earl of Douglas with a fine prospect of the rich farmlands of Northumberland, which stretch south from here towards the Tyne valley. (Author's photo)

drove road, as far as Rothley Crags, where he turned due south. It may be that the Scots who 'lyghted down' upon Greenleighton, which is about one-and-a-half miles north of the drove road across Ottercops Moss, were outriders of the main body or a separate column of horsemen that had taken a more northerly route from the neighbourhood of Rochester, along the line of the Roman Road, and then across Davyshiel Common, skirting Elsdon to the north; a route that would have brought them to Greenleighton. Two small columns of troops will always travel faster than one large one, so we can be in no doubt that the Scots progressed in this manner when the terrain allowed, 'riding at a good pace, through bye-roads without attacking town, castle or house', for they had determined to enter Durham before they began their work of destruction. They crossed the River Tyne 'about three leagues above Newcastle', which may be at Ovingham, or above Newburn, or below the Umfravilles' castle of Prudhoe, which stands guard high above the river crossing.

The Scots' advance was rapid, perhaps even matching Froissart's 'sixty to seventy miles in a day and night', though this is an astonishing speed that could not be sustained for long; yet, with fresh horses, in the first 36 hours of their invasion Douglas' force was able to strike deep into County Durham. The Scots did not delay to plunder or burn the scattered farmsteads and villages of Northumberland that lay in their path, but advanced the 40 miles from the Redeswire to the River Tyne with only a minimum of halts; they crossed the river and rode unopposed into the rich and populous palatinate of Durham. Only at this point did the Scots begin their war, burning villages and slaying the inhabitants, leaving a swathe of destruction in their wake as they advanced, on a broad front, towards the city of Durham. It was reported at the time that some of the raiders advanced even to the gates of York, though it is probable that this refers to the Durham–Yorkshire boundary, rather than to the city of York itself.

The English were caught by surprise by the speed of Douglas' advance, and the savagery of his onslaught convinced them that the whole might of the Scottish army had descended upon them; the county was ablaze from end to end before they belatedly responded. Hotspur, the warden of the East March, and his brother Ralph had left the defence of the castles of Alnwick and Warkworth in the hands of their father, the earl of Northumberland; forewarned of Scottish intentions, they had ridden with a strong body of men-at-arms and archers to Newcastle, where they had concentrated their forces, intending to strike back at the Scots when the time came. The defences of the main towns and castles of Northumberland and Durham were in a good state of preparedness; the walls of Newcastle had recently been completed at great expense, but this did not prevent the highly mobile Scots sweeping across County Durham, striking terror into the inhabitants and destroying everything in their path.

In mid-July, well aware of the threat of a Scottish invasion, Richard II had sent letters to the lords of the northern Marches, bidding them await the arrival of himself with his forces, and those of the earl of Arundel, who had been recalled from operations in French waters. The king's instructions acted as a constraint on the actions of the northern lords, who might otherwise have made a more active response to

**THE ENCOUNTER OUTSIDE THE WALLS OF NEWCASTLE
BETWEEN HOTSPUR AND THE EARL OF DOUGLAS**
(pages 42–43)

Froissart's *Chronicles* is the only source that mentions the
duel between Hotspur and the earl of Douglas:

> ... they [the Scots] returned to Newcastle and there
> rested and tarried two days, and every day they
> scrimmished. The earl of Northumberland's two sons
> were two young lusty knights and were ever foremost
> at the barriers to scrimmish. There were many proper
> feats of arms done and achieved: there was fighting
> hand to hand: among other there fought hand to hand
> the earl of Douglas and sir Henry Percy, and by force
> of arms the earl of Douglas won the pennon of sir
> Henry Percy's, wherewith he was sore displeased and
> so were all the Englishmen.

The medieval town walls of Newcastle-upon-Tyne, and the
great West Gate, form the backdrop to the famous duel. In
the distance stands the castle keep, built in the reign of
Henry II, who resumed possession of Northumberland from

the Scots and built the New Castle, from which the town
takes its name. The town walls were built during the reign
of Edward I, with later additions to provide protection for the
townsfolk against the marauding Scots. The burgesses paid
a wall tax or murage for their upkeep; nevertheless they fell
into disrepair and a fine was imposed by Edward III. The
antiquarian John Leland, writing in Henry VIII's time, said that
the strength and magnificence of the walling of the town far
surpassed all the walls of the cities of England and most of
the towns of Europe. They proved an impenetrable barrier
to the Scots and it was not until 1644, during the Civil War,
that the town was taken. The fortifications consisted of a
wall 20ft high with a crenellated parapet and a wall walk
accessible only from the towers and gateways that it linked
together; outside was a deep ditch or moat 60ft wide. The
complete circuit of the walls was over two miles in length
and there were originally six gateways and 18 towers; the
West Gate, from whose towers fly the banners of the earl
of Northumberland (1), and St George of England (2), was
so massive as to be a fortress in itself, and was later
strengthened by the addition of a barbican. Today only two
stretches of the ramparts still stand; the gateways have all
gone, and of the towers only seven remain.

An impressive section of the medieval walls of Newcastle-upon-Tyne survives to the north of the site of the great West Gate. This view from the Herber Tower looks north-east towards Morden Tower, one of seven towers and turrets that still stand today. (Author's illustration)

Douglas' invasion: in the event, neither Arundel nor the king appeared in the north that year.

After a brief skirmish outside Durham, the Scots turned north, burning and ravaging the countryside as they withdrew towards the Tyne burdened with so rich a haul of plunder that it slowed their progress to that of an army on foot.

THE SCOTS AT THE GATES OF NEWCASTLE

The Scots re-crossed the River Tyne at the same point they had used during their advance and boldly marched east along the north bank to Newcastle, where they halted and set up camp before the recently completed fortifications of the West Gate. The English imagined, as the Scots surely intended, that Douglas' force was only the Scottish vanguard, and that the earl of Fife was lurking nearby with the main body of the Scottish host, waiting for them to take the bait proffered and sally out into a trap. The town was crammed with troops, not only the Percys' following, but also those of Sir Mathew Redman, governor of Berwick; the seneschal of York; Sir Ralph Lumley; Sir Robert Ogle; Sir Thomas Grey, and many other worthy northern knights who were gathered within the walls.

There was almost continual skirmishing between the two sides during the time that Douglas lay outside the town, though the defenders declined to risk a full-scale encounter. Froissart recounts a tale that we can take either at face value or as a literary device introduced to point up the chivalric nature of the conflict between Douglas and Percy that, as he saw it, was to result in the battle of Otterburn. During one of these skirmishes at the barriers outside the West Gate, the earl of Douglas and Hotspur met and engaged in single combat; Hotspur had the worst of the encounter, and his lance pennon was taken by the Scot. The Scots expected to be attacked in their camp that very night but were disappointed, as Hotspur was persuaded by less impetuous counsel to defer his attempt to recover the pennon.

Whether or not Froissart's tale of the duel between Percy and Douglas is true, it does appear that an element of personal rivalry between the two leaders surfaced at Newcastle. The *Westminster Chronicle*

LEFT, TOP **The Umfravilles' fortress at Prudhoe occupies a strong site, on a steep spur, high above the crossings of the river Tyne. Though this was impregnable to the earl of Douglas' army, the garrison could do nothing to prevent the Scots from crossing the river below. (Author's photo)**

LEFT, BOTTOM **Warkworth Castle came into the hands of the Percys in 1332. The surviving fabric is ruined but otherwise much as it would have been in Hotspur's day. (Photo, Keith Durham)**

ABOVE **The first earl of Northumberland extensively strengthened the defences of Warkworth in the 1380s and had his arms and crest set high on the wall of the Lion Tower. (Photo, Keith Durham)**

relates that Hotspur replied to an abusive message from Douglas at Newcastle with an 'undertaking that before it was Douglas's fortune to reach Scotland the pair would certainly meet'. Under cover of darkness, before dawn, on the day preceding the battle of Otterburn, the Scots decamped and headed homeward. The safety of the livestock and plunder they had lifted in England had been ensured by despatching it previously, well ahead of the army.

THE SCOTS WITHDRAW TO OTTERBURN

The Scots took the road north-west from Newcastle, which took them through Ponteland, about seven miles distant, before sunrise, where they surprised and burnt the castle and town and took prisoner Sir Raymond Delaval. We do not know the route that the Scots took from Ponteland to Otterburn, and there are no records of Scottish depredation to provide clues; even Elsdon, a village of some local importance, records no damage at this time. The earl of Douglas' force covered the 31 miles from Newcastle on horseback, unencumbered by any slow-moving carts and livestock, which, as suggested earlier, they had despatched ahead of them. It is possible that one of the reasons for Douglas' impudent bluff outside Newcastle was to give his plunder a head start; militarily this makes more sense than the suggestion that he intended to attack the strongly held fortified town with his small force. Had the Scots started for home encumbered by their plunder their rate of progress would have been slow and they would have risked being caught in the open countryside by the English cavalry, at a great disadvantage. By the evening before the day of battle, the Scots had established themselves in strongly positioned encampments in Redesdale, just a mile beyond Otterburn.

HOTSPUR PURSUES THE SCOTS

When the scouts despatched to tail the withdrawing Scots reported to Hotspur, it became apparent that Douglas had deluded him; he realized that the main Scottish army was in the West March, and that the earl was already a day's march ahead of him. Hotspur was stung into action; his reputation and honour were at stake, and he resolved to pursue the Scots with all his available strength. A day's march to the south, the bishop of Durham was toiling towards Newcastle with his levies, to reinforce Hotspur. It was not rashness, but rather a cool realization that there was not a moment to waste if he was to catch Douglas, that prompted Hotspur to march without awaiting the lord bishop's arrival.

Froissart, in stating that the Percys left Newcastle after dinner, that is, in the early afternoon rather than on the morning of the day of battle, was clearly mistaken. He believed that Otterburn was 'eight short leagues distant', which is 16 miles, and that the reason why Hotspur arrived there so late in the day was that his infantry slowed the advance. In fact, Otterburn is 31 miles from Newcastle and there was no possibility of fully armed infantry marching so far in a day; normally they covered only half that distance in a good day's march. The probability is that Hotspur's force did not include infantry at all, but was made up entirely of mounted troops; only horsemen could traverse the rough tracks between Newcastle and Otterburn in a day.

Hotspur's long column of troops, with their laden pack animals, snaked beneath the towers of Newcastle's great West Gate on the morning of the fateful day and rode north-west, following in the wake of the Scots. The heavily armed horsemen advanced at the best pace that the nags of the mounted infantry could be persuaded to adopt over a distance of 31 miles. If this was, as seems probable, no more than four miles an hour, then, allowing for delays and rests en route, it would take about ten hours to ride to Otterburn. If we further suppose that the

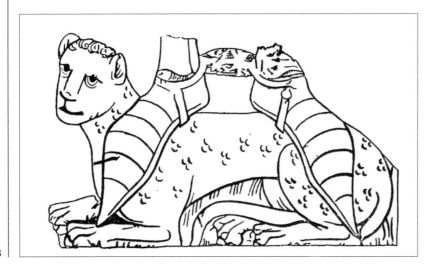

Only the feet of the once fine monumental brass of Aymer de Athol, lord of Ponteland, who died in 1402, survive today. According to Froissart, the Scots '... came to a castle called Pontland, whereof sir Edmund of Alphel was lord, who was a right good knight ... and gave a great assault, so that by force of arms they won it and the knight within it. Then the town and castle was brent.'

The castle of Newcastle-upon-Tyne stands today surrounded by urban clutter and hemmed in by the railway. The castle originally stood in a walled enclosure and guarded the bridge over the River Tyne below. (Photo, Keith Durham)

column of riders left Newcastle at the not unreasonable hour of 9am, then they would arrive in Redesdale about 7pm. Sunset in northern England in early August 1388 would have been around 8pm, so Hotspur would have had no time to lose if he was to bring the Scots to battle in the last hour of daylight. Hardyng confirms that the battle began before sundown, saying that Douglas launched his attack against the English flank 'Rycht at the Swnnys downe-gangyng'; and, similarly, Walter Bower describes the banners of the Scots 'glowing in the reflection of the sun's rays a little before it set'.

THE SCOTS AT OTTERBURN

Early in the morning of the day of battle, the Scots launched an unsuccessful assault on the castle at Otterburn, a fortification that was in those days 'tolerably strong and situated among marshes'. This fortification stood in the village, beside the road, on the left bank of the Otter Burn. There is evidence for the existence of a fortification here as early as 1245; possibly the 'capital messuage' referred to in the will of Gilbert de Umfraville in 1308. Despairing of taking the castle, the Scottish leaders held a council of war to decide upon a course of action. The majority were for abandoning the attack on the castle and decamping on the morrow, but Douglas overruled them and declared that honour was doubly served by remaining, not only to renew the assault on the castle, but to allow Hotspur time to come to reclaim his pennon. The chivalric motive suggested by Froissart for Douglas' decision to obligingly await Hotspur at Otterburn makes little military sense. It is possible that his dalliance in the area was in order to burn and pillage a locality left untouched, due to the rapidity of his earlier advance. If this is so, then he must have been confident that he could deal with Hotspur if he were to show up in Redesdale.

THE BATTLE OF OTTERBURN, AUGUST 1388

MEDIEVAL WRITTEN SOURCES

The 'Cavers Ensign' is traditionally held to be the standard of James, Earl of Douglas, and to have been carried at Otterburn by his natural son Archibald Douglas, ancestor of the house of Cavers. The flag has been the subject of much argument and is discussed fully in *PSAS* vol. 36, 1901–02. (Author's illustration)

Of all the battles that have been described in this history, great and small, this of which I am now speaking was the best fought and the most severe; for there was not a man, knight or squire, who did not acquit himself gallantly, hand to hand with the enemy.

Froissart, *Chronicles*

Pitched battles were rare events in border warfare and the battle of Otterburn was widely reported at the time. Eight medieval accounts have survived. The most famous version is that of Jean Froissart of Hainault (*c*.1337–1410), who was in the entourage of Edward III and Queen Phillipa, herself a Hainaulter from 1361 to 1369. During this time he visited Scotland where he spent two weeks at Dalkeith, in the household of William, Earl of Douglas, father of the Sir James Douglas who fell at Otterburn, who was then a child. In 1389 he met, at Orthez, two Gascon esquires, Jean de Cantiran and Jean de Castelnau, who had fought in Hotspur's retinue in the battle, and later the same year, at Avignon, he encountered a Scottish knight and two esquires of the household of the earl of Douglas who had also fought at Otterburn. From the stories of these five participants Froissart wrote his own colourful version of the battle.

The *Westminster Chronicle* covers the years 1381–94. The author's narrative of the battle of Otterburn may derive from the account of a participant; it was written down shortly after the events described, no later than 1391.

Thomas Walsingham, author of the *Historia Anglicana*, was a monk of St Albans. His version of the invasion of 1388 is highly partisan and short on reliable facts.

Henry Knighton was a monk of St Mary's Abbey, Leicester, who chronicled the years 1337–96. His narrative of the Otterburn War is not the most informative part of his chronicle. Both Knighton and Walsingham were propagandists, who exaggerated Scottish losses to minimize the English defeat.

John Hardyng wrote his *Chronicle* about 50 years after the battle. He entered the service of Hotspur in 1390, aged 12, and later became his esquire. He fought at the battle of Shrewsbury where Hotspur was killed. Shortly afterwards he took service with Sir Robert Umfraville, Lord of Redesdale, and fought in his company at Agincourt. He must have heard accounts of the battle of Otterburn from both Hotspur and Sir Robert, who, according to Hardyng, played an important part in the battle.

Looking north-east across Redesdale from Dere Street to the eminence of Blakeman's Law. The farm of Greenchesters is lit by sunlight below the dark block of trees in right centre of the picture. On the right the land slopes away towards Otterburn village. (Author's photo)

The *Orygynale Cronykil* of Scotland, by Andrew Wyntoun, the prior of St Serf's isle in Loch Leven, incorporates a section from an anonymous source, including an account of the battle of Otterburn, written shortly after the battle, some 20 years before the rest of the chronicle was completed.

The *Scotichronicon* was written by Walter Bower in the 1440s, while he was abbot of Inchcolm in the Firth of Forth. It contains a chapter based on the same anonymous informant as that used by Wyntoun. The *Scotichronicon* also includes a poem on the battle by Thomas Barry, short on information though epic in length.

THE SITE OF THE BATTLE OF OTTERBURN

Medieval chronicles are reticent regarding topographic detail and the sources we have for the battle of Otterburn are no exception. Neither the Scottish nor the English chroniclers are expansive, mentioning only Otterburn, Redesdale or the River Rede; Walsingham does not mention a location at all. Knighton confuses matters by saying that the battle was fought near 'Zolston', which must be Elsdon. Froissart says that the battle was fought 'between Newcastle and Otterburn', that is, to the east of the village, thus echoing Knighton, and adding support to the idea of an alternative battle site near Elsdon. The traditional site of the battle, which best fits the known facts, is known as Battle Riggs or Battle Croft; it lies a short distance past Otterburn, on the road up Redesdale, and is marked by an obelisk called Percy's Cross.

THE DATE OF THE BATTLE OF OTTERBURN

It is generally agreed that the battle of Otterburn took place in the month of August 1388; however, there is less accord regarding the exact day of the month on which the battle was fought. The English and Scottish chroniclers do not dissent from 5 August as the day of battle; however Froissart dates the battle later, on Wednesday 19 August. Support for this later date revolves around the fact that there would have been light from an almost full moon on 19 August; this would not have been the case on the 5th, when there would have been a new moon, providing little light by which to fight a battle. If we turn to the chroniclers we find no mention of either a full moon or a new moon, though there is ample confirmation of the confusion brought about by the darkness. The Westminster chronicler noted that '... the darkness played such tricks on the English that when they aimed a careless blow at a Scotsman, owing to the chorus of voices speaking a single language it was an Englishman that they cut down.'

THE SCOTS FORTIFY THEMSELVES AT OTTERBURN

At a council of war, called by Douglas, after the failure of the attack on Otterburn Castle, the earl overruled the majority of his chiefs, who were for decamping, in favour of remaining at Otterburn. Froissart continues the story: '... they returned to their quarters. They made huts of trees and branches and strongly fortified themselves.' The context strongly suggests that the chronicler meant that it was the Scottish leaders and fighting men who returned and fortified their camp, for he goes on to say that 'They placed their baggage and servants at the entrance of the marsh on the road to Newcastle and the cattle they drove into the marsh lands.' In other words, the servants were encamped in a separate place to guard the cattle and plunder. There is no doubt that the men-at-arms and knights would not have wanted to share the midge-infested valley bottom with the servants and livestock. That there were indeed two separate camps is borne out in a later passage in Froissart, when he describes a body of Scottish troops being sent to reinforce the servants' camp, in order to gain time for the Scottish knights and men-at-arms, who were hastily arming themselves elsewhere. Many of the so-called servants were youths who attended to the army's horses when they encamped for the night or when battle was joined, and, though not armoured and equipped to take their place in the fighting line, they carried weapons to defend themselves and were present in substantial numbers.

> he that had a bonnie boy
> Sent out his horse to grass;
> And he that had not a bonnie boy
> His ain servant he was.
>
> Sir Walter Scott, *The Battle of Otterburn*

There was a good deal of marshland in that part of the valley of the Rede in which the servants made their camp; this is evident from Froissart's description of its being 'at the entrance of the marsh on the road to Newcastle'. In medieval times Redesdale supported an abundant

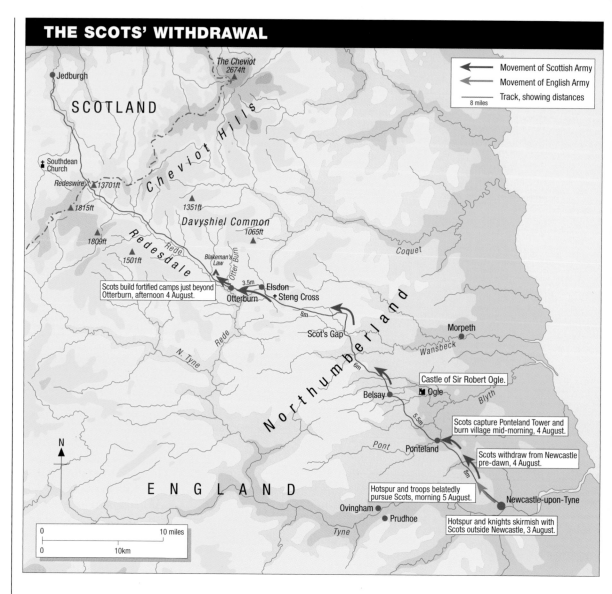

Movement of Scottish Army
Movement of English Army
Track, showing distances
8 miles

Jedburgh

The Cheviot 2674ft

SCOTLAND

Cheviot Hills

Southdean Church
Redeswire · 1370 1ft
· 1815ft

1351ft

Davyshiel Common
1065ft

Coquet

· 1809ft
Redesdale
Rede
Otter Burn
1501ft
Blakeman's Law

Scots build fortified camps just beyond Otterburn, afternoon 4 August.

3.5m
Otterburn
Elsdon
Steng Cross

8m

Scot's Gap

Northumberland

Morpeth
Wansbeck

N. Tyne
Rede

6m

Belsay

Ogle

Castle of Sir Robert Ogle.

Blyth

Scots capture Ponteland Tower and burn village mid-morning, 4 August.

5.5m

N

Pont
Ponteland

Scots withdraw from Newcastle pre-dawn, 4 August.

ENGLAND

8m

Hotspur and troops belatedly pursue Scots, morning 5 August.

Ovingham
Prudhoe

Newcastle-upon-Tyne

Tyne

Hotspur and knights skirmish with Scots outside Newcastle, 3 August.

0 —————————— 10 miles
0 —————————— 10km

variety of vegetation; birch, rowan, alder and hazel crowded along the watercourses and gathered in more isolated stands and coppices on the upland slopes. The earliest detailed map of the area, drawn by Captain Armstrong in 1769, shows woodland in the area beyond the 'Battle Stone' and below the old fort on Blakeman's Law. There are some large birches standing even today on the flank of the hill, and it is readily apparent from these that the more abundant medieval woodland would have concealed the movements of the Scots from an enemy approaching from the direction of Otterburn. The fortifications that the Scots constructed were probably no more than a reinforcing of the existing trees and undergrowth with fallen timber and cut branches, rather than earthworks; nevertheless this would have made their camps places of some strength. The servants' encampment may have had additional protection from the marshes, which flanked the river in this area and protected their front to some extent. Their camp probably straddled the track above the left bank of the river where it loops

The farm of Greenchesters from Blakeman's Law. The loop in the river beyond the farmhouse encloses a flat area where the Scottish servants watched over the plundered livestock and horses. The narrow neck of land between the farm and the river may be the site of the fortification that the Scots built across the road, which can be seen running behind Greenchesters. Reinforcements were sent to the servants down the slope in the foreground from the camp of the men-at-arms above. (Author's photo)

northwards below Greenchesters. Upstream from this location there is a wide expanse of valley bottom, which must have been the marshland where the cattle and horses were driven for safekeeping. It was not intended that the servants should hold this position alone; it was an integral part of the Scottish defences, and the defence was intended to be stiffened by a body of men-at-arms in case of attack. However, as the Scots were taken by surprise, the men-at-arms were still arming themselves some distance away when the attackers broke into the servants' camp. The knights and men-at-arms were encamped on the higher ground, above the marshland, near the remains of the ancient British fort on the shoulder of Blakeman's Law. It is doubtful whether these remains, now barely discernible as a feature of the landscape, would have amounted to much more in the 14th century, so it cannot be assumed that these slight earthworks played any part in the selection of a site for the main Scottish camp. The best we can say about it is that it was not too far removed from that of the servants and that, as subsequent events show, it was on Blakeman's Law, above Greenchesters. The Scottish fighting men were well positioned on the high ground to observe Hotspur's advance along the track up Redesdale and to threaten and fall upon his flank if the opportunity presented itself. Alternatively, if the English came along the drove road that ran two miles to the north, from the neighbourhood of Elsdon, over Davyshiel Common, and almost parallel to the track up Redesdale, then the Scots were well placed to deal with an advance from that direction too.

As the shadows lengthened, the Scots became increasingly confident that Hotspur would not arrive that day, their scouts having brought no word of his approach; as the afternoon wore on, the men-at-arms disarmed and rested, and some slept while others turned their thoughts towards their supper. The tranquillity was rudely shattered by the arrival, pell-mell, of a rider, whose shrill call to arms awoke the Scots to their danger; the enemy were upon them; they had been taken by surprise. It is difficult to account for this other than by suggesting that it was due to the unexpected rapidity of Hotspur's advance, and that the Scots were let down by their scouts; certainly Barry thought so: 'They send out no patrols whatever, of higher or lower rank … they are found wanting.'

In contrast, the following day, the Scottish scouts were on good form; Froissart tells us that the Scots knew that the bishop of Durham had left Newcastle before he had advanced two leagues and that this intelligence was confirmed by their scouts. It is possible that the Scots did send their scouts out and that they were spotted and ridden down by well-mounted English outriders forming a screen ahead of the main body of troops. Hotspur's advance into Redesdale from the south-east would have been screened from the view of the Scots on Blakeman's Law by Fawdon Hill; they would not have caught sight of the English until they emerged from the village of Otterburn.

The sun was setting ever lower in the west as Hotspur and his weary troops, having spent the whole day fully armed in the saddle, descended towards Elsdon. Hotspur's scouts had informed him that the Scots were still encamped near Otterburn and he had formed a plan of attack with his officers. The English may have paused awhile near Elsdon to regroup and allow the long tail of the column to come up with the leading troops. From the village there were two possible lines of approach to the Scottish position beyond Otterburn. One possibility was the drove road that rises from Elsdon and runs north-west over Davyshiel Common, though an attack against the Scots' camp above Greenchesters from that direction would mean advancing across two miles of rough, boggy moorland. An army approaching the Scottish position from an easterly

Below the windswept summit of Blakeman's Law is a more sheltered shoulder where the Scottish men-at-arms made their camp. The ruins of the pele of Shittlehaugh stand here high above Redesdale and command the road that leads north-west to the border at Carter Bar. (Author's photo)

direction could not have fallen upon the servants' camp without first of all encountering that of the men-at-arms. Hotspur must have realized that it was more direct and far quicker to approach the Scots along the level track from Elsdon, through Otterburn into Redesdale.

Hotspur was aware of the urgency of mounting an immediate attack on the Scots, and in order to maximize the element of surprise he sent the vanguard of the army, commanded by Sir Mathew Redman, straight into action, while he waited until the main body of his troops came up. Redman and his men rode along the track up Redesdale and dismounted, letting loose their horses at the last moment, before furiously assaulting the camp that blocked their way. They quickly fought their way in but did not realize that this was only the servants' camp rather than that of their masters. Nevertheless, the camp in the valley bottom proved strong enough to check the English assault for a short while, giving the Scottish men-at-arms time to arm themselves in their own camp above. They sent a body of men to reinforce the lower camp where the servants' resistance was crumbling, and these reinforcements kept up the fight on this part of the field. The Westminster chronicler considered that the purpose of Redman's attack was to take the enemy in the rear and throw them into confusion while Hotspur launched a frontal assault, though he is infuriatingly vague about where Redman's attack took place, saying only that it was 'on the enemy's other side'. Hardyng similarly says that Hotspur sent Redman 'beyond the Scots', that is, to outflank them, and adds that this was to prevent their escape.

Wyntoun relates that many of the Scottish men-at-arms donned their armour in such haste that their arming was incomplete and parts of their harness, cuisses (armour for protecting the front of the thighs), greaves and even vambraces (armour for the forearms) were omitted. The earl of Moray could not find his bascinet in the chaos and fought bareheaded. Douglas himself, with little concern for his own safety, was carelessly armed as he furiously set about arraying his men for battle. Fortunately for the Scots, they had a pre-arranged plan, which was to be the saving of them, as the confusion occasioned by their being surprised could easily have led to disorderly defeat. But the Scots knew exactly what to do in their predicament and the dangerous situation was restored to order.

Meanwhile the main body of the English army was arriving piecemeal in the area near the present Percy's Cross. Despite knowing that it would be some time before the tail end of his troops arrived, Hotspur dismounted the men available, and, scarcely bothering to form them into battle order, signalled the advance. As the monk of Westminster puts it, they 'straggled into action in irregular order'; Barry describes them 'advancing hastily and in no order' and adds that one side of the battle line was composed of men-at-arms bunched together, and on the other side was placed a company of archers. They advanced boldly, though 'in the disorder induced by haste', on a broad front, their left flank towards the River Rede, their right flank, in the air, on the slopes of the long, low ridge that ran down from the higher ground beyond Greenchesters.

And so, with great imagination
Proper to madmen, led his powers to death,
And, winking, leap'd into destruction.

Shakespeare, *Henry IV Part I* | **57**

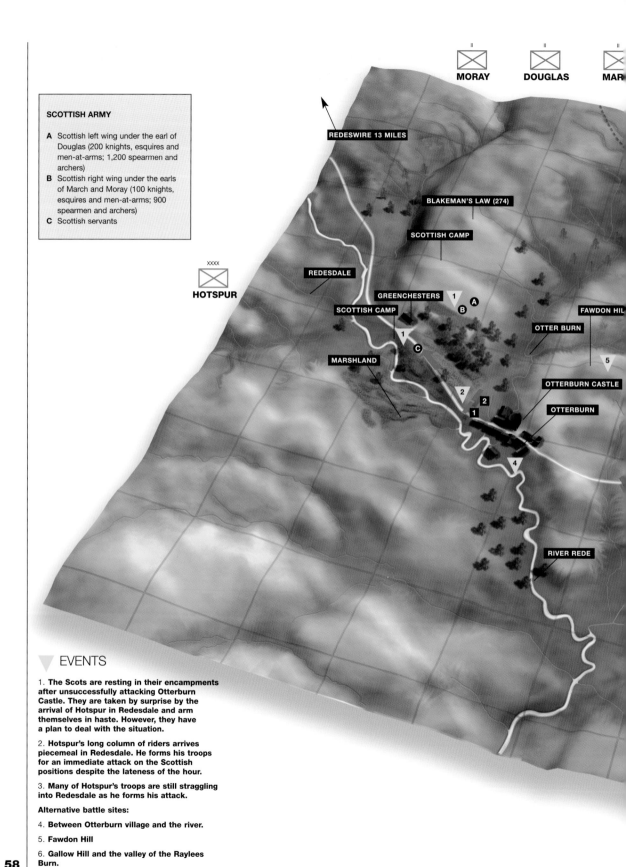

MORAY **DOUGLAS** **MAR**

SCOTTISH ARMY

A Scottish left wing under the earl of Douglas (200 knights, esquires and men-at-arms; 1,200 spearmen and archers)

B Scottish right wing under the earls of March and Moray (100 knights, esquires and men-at-arms; 900 spearmen and archers)

C Scottish servants

HOTSPUR

REDESWIRE 13 MILES

BLAKEMAN'S LAW (274)

SCOTTISH CAMP

REDESDALE

GREENCHESTERS

SCOTTISH CAMP

FAWDON HILL

OTTER BURN

MARSHLAND

OTTERBURN CASTLE

OTTERBURN

RIVER REDE

▼ EVENTS

1. **The Scots are resting in their encampments after unsuccessfully attacking Otterburn Castle. They are taken by surprise by the arrival of Hotspur in Redesdale and arm themselves in haste. However, they have a plan to deal with the situation.**

2. **Hotspur's long column of riders arrives piecemeal in Redesdale. He forms his troops for an immediate attack on the Scottish positions despite the lateness of the hour.**

3. **Many of Hotspur's troops are still straggling into Redesdale as he forms his attack.**

Alternative battle sites:

4. **Between Otterburn village and the river.**

5. **Fawdon Hill**

6. **Gallow Hill and the valley of the Raylees Burn.**

THE BATTLE OF OTTERBURN

5 August 1388, Hotspur and his troops surprise the Scots in Redesdale in the late afternoon.

Note: Gridlines are marked at 1km/0.62 miles. Hill heights are given in brackets and measured in metres.

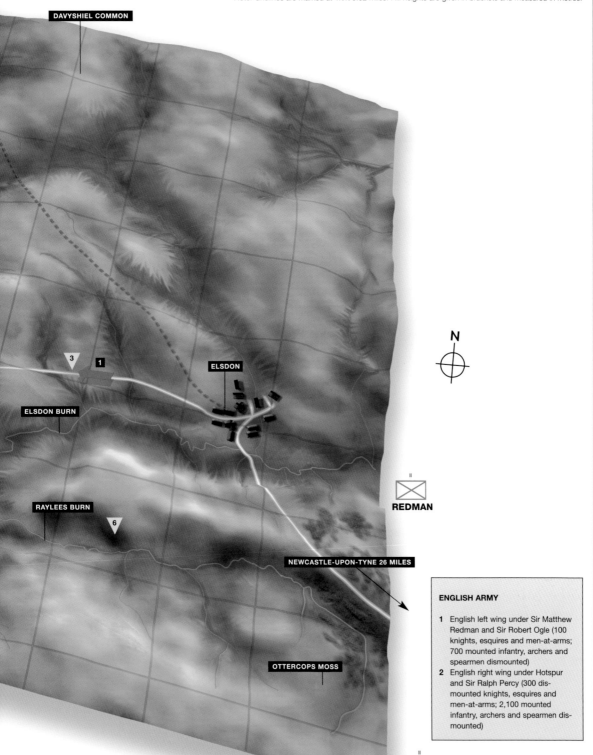

DAVYSHIEL COMMON

3

1

ELSDON

ELSDON BURN

RAYLEES BURN

6

REDMAN

NEWCASTLE-UPON-TYNE 26 MILES

OTTERCOPS MOSS

OGLE

ENGLISH ARMY

1 English left wing under Sir Matthew Redman and Sir Robert Ogle (100 knights, esquires and men-at-arms; 700 mounted infantry, archers and spearmen dismounted)

2 English right wing under Hotspur and Sir Ralph Percy (300 dismounted knights, esquires and men-at-arms; 2,100 mounted infantry, archers and spearmen dismounted)

THE EARL OF DOUGLAS COUNTER-ATTACKS

The Scots formed up, however incomplete their arming, under the banners of their commanders and left the camp on the shoulder of Blakeman's Law silently. They did not advance directly towards the oncoming English, who were by then probably above and level with the present school. The Scots may have used a slight depression that runs behind the crest of the shoulder of Blakeman's Law, at the northern end of the south-east ridge, to conceal their movement onto the flank of the English, who were advancing north-west, up the ridge. However, the depression can only have been of limited use, because it runs almost due east; following it for any distance would take the Scots further from the enemy rather than onto their flank. The south-east ridge is really no more than a gentle swelling of the landscape between the valley of the River Rede and that of the Otter Burn. From the valley bottom the ridge appears to rise to a summit crest, but this is not the case when viewed from the position of the Scottish camp above Greenchesters. As the ridge has no crest as such, its gentle, almost flat profile offers no cover for an enemy to approach unseen from the concealment of dead ground. There are still residual groups of tall birch on the upper part of the ridge today, and these suggest the truth about the surprise achieved by Douglas' flanking movement, for, as Froissart relates, they 'fell on the enemy's flank quite unexpectedly, shouting their cries'. The trees, bushes and undergrowth, which were more abundant on the ridge in those days, rather than the lie of the land, hid the Scots and allowed them to launch a surprise attack on the English flank. Wyntoun's version of events describes Earl James' approach and supports this proposition:

View down the shallow south-east ridge of Blakeman's Law towards Otterburn. The trees in the foreground serve as reminders that in the 14th century the abundant vegetation on the ridge allowed the Scots to approach unseen and take Hotspur by surprise. (Author's photo)

Panorama of the battlefield from the position of the Scottish men-at-arms' camp on Blakeman's Law. Hotspur's attack was launched up the low ridge, probably just right of centre, and was taken in flank by the Scots emerging from cover on the left of the picture. (Author's photo)

Towart his Fays the nerrast way,
Qwhare Buskis ware, as I herd say,
Qwahare Inglis men saw noucht his cummyng;

The Scots approached Hotspur's oncoming troops first by moving some way along the depression mentioned earlier, then by moving south, before wheeling onto the English flank. As soon as the Scots broke cover and emerged from the friendly concealment of the woods, they paused a short moment to order their ranks and unfurled their banners. Then, with mighty war cries, they fell furiously on the flank of the ragged formation of astonished English troops, who were overwhelmed by the impetus of the Scots before they could organize themselves to check the assault. The speed with which the Scots closed with the disorganized English bowmen, and the wrath of their onset, denied the archers time to wreak the havoc that Douglas, who knew their fearful reputation, had so feared.

The English right wing was severely mauled before Hotspur brought up more troops to stabilize the situation; then, lit by the last rays of the sun as it sank below the western horizon, the battle developed into a bloody scrum as both sides strained to thrust back the other at push of pike. Now that the armies were closely engaged the bows of the archers were useless, and they could only take up what weapons they had and add their weight to the struggling masses of spearmen. Froissart is in his element describing the feats of arms of the knights on both sides as the fighting raged on into the twilight. Although Wyntoun says that the armies 'fought right stoutly all the night', the serious fighting cannot have lasted long after sunset, and we may be absolved for treating his statement as an exaggeration used for dramatic effect. The day-long ride from Newcastle must have told against the English in the desperate hand-to-hand struggle; Hotspur had placed his reliance on the element of surprise, and when the battle turned into a slogging match, the well-fed and rested Scots had the advantage over his weary troops. The confusion of the mêlée is matched by that of the chroniclers over this phase of the fighting, making it difficult to be positive about the sequence of events that led to Hotspur's defeat. What is certain is that

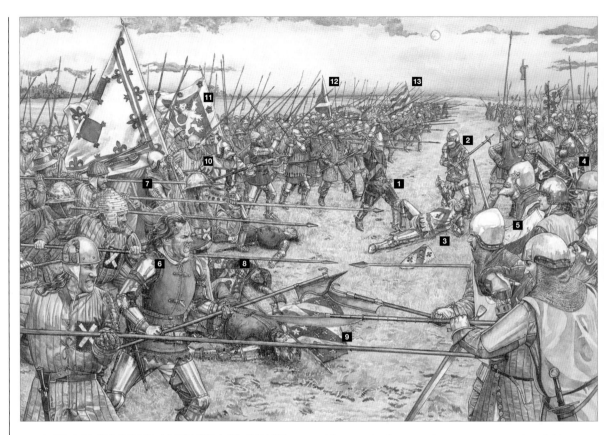

THE BATTLE OF OTTERBURN. AS THE SUN SETS THE TIDE OF BATTLE TURNS; THE ONSLAUGHT OF THE EARLS OF MARCH AND MORAY CAUSES THE ENGLISH LINE TO GIVE WAY. (pages 62–63)

Walter Bower, in his *Scotichronicon*, provides the detail that allows us to illustrate the drama of the moment during the battle of Otterburn when the English line began to crumble:

> When therefore they had begun to do battle, suddenly a certain especially doughty and powerful knight, the Scot John Swinton, leapt out from the flank of the battle line, and as both sides were assailing each other with lances, he withdrew sideways a little from both sides, raised his terrible long lance energetically, struck the iron tips of many English lances from the side, and knocked them to the ground with each blow. As a result the Scots were the first to strike home on the English with their lances, and with powerful force compelled them willy-nilly to withdraw.

Sir John, right centre (1), can be identified by the canting arms of Swinton displayed on his *jupon* or surcoat. He wields a mighty polearm and is about to strike down Sir Ralph Percy (2), who was badly wounded in the battle. Sir Ralph stands over the fallen Sir John Copledyke (3), who raises a hand as a token of surrender. Other knights on the English side who can be identified by their arms are Sir John Lilburn (4) and Sir William Hilton (5). Sir William, whose brother Sir Thomas was also captured at Otterburn, had great difficulty raising his ransom. He fought at Humbleton Hill in 1402 where he reversed his fortunes, building Hilton Castle from the proceeds of Scottish ransoms. In the left foreground, the earl of Moray (6), bareheaded, leads his motley spearmen forward; his banner is carried by Sir Patrick Hepburn of Hailes (7). The earl of Douglas (8) lies dead with his trusty esquires beside him where they fell, defending the earl's banner (9). Sir Thomas Erskine (10) was, according to Wyntoun, 'Fellely wondyt in the face'. In the Scottish fighting line beyond is displayed the banner of George Dunbar, Earl of March (11), who altered his allegiance in 1400 and fought on the English side at Humbleton Hill. The Scottish national flag (12) bears the arms of St Andrew; the Scots wore his cross as a badge from an early date often sewn to a black backing. In the distance flies the banner of Sir Malcolm Drummond (13).

the earl of Douglas was killed in the midst of the desperate and bloody struggle; though, as neither side at the time was aware of his death, the loss of the Scottish leader had no influence on the outcome of the battle.

THE EARL OF MARCH TIPS THE SCALES

After the initial shock of the Scottish onslaught, the English rallied and brought up reinforcements; their superior numbers might have been beginning to tell against the Scots when Douglas was killed. The turning point of the battle was the timely intervention in the mêlée of the earl of March, who, according to Walsingham, brought fresh troops 'in overwhelming strength' from 'another part of the field'. This tipped the scales in favour of the Scots and led to the English collapse. Froissart's dramatic account gives the mortally wounded Douglas a role in defeating the English before he expires, telling how the earl called for his banner to be raised again, as his banner bearer had been killed; then the cry of 'Douglas!' rallied the Scots to his banner. Intertwined with Froissart's imaginative tale of Douglas' death is the bland, though significant, statement that 'The earls of Moray and March, with their banners and men, came thither also', which adds more weight to the evidence for its being March and his brother Moray's intervention that turned the tide in favour of the Scots.

Walter Bower heard a different version of events; he gives the credit for breaking the English line to Sir John Swinton, a famous fighter cast in the heroic mould, whose furious assault on the enemy tipped the balance (see caption opposite).

It seems probable that Hotspur committed his reinforcements piecemeal to the fray as they tailed in; whereas March, whose subsequent career proved him one of the best military commanders of his time, launched a concerted attack on a vulnerable part of the English line, bringing to bear the pressure that caused their collapse.

SCOTTISH ARMY

A Earl of March's contingent
B Scottish left wing under earl of
   Douglas
C Infantry reinforcements
D Scottish camp servants

MARCH

BLAKEMAN'S LAW (274)

SCOTTISH CAMP

OLD FORT (217)

FORTIFIC
OF WOO
UNDERG

REDESWIRE 13 MILES

REDESDALE

GREENCHESTERS

SITE OF M
SCHO

DERE STREET ROMAN ROAD

SCOTTISH
SERVANTS' CAMP

 EVENTS

1. **Troops still straggle into Redesdale as Hotspur attacks.**

2. **PHASE ONE: Hotspur launches a disorganized attack towards the Scottish camps. He sends Sir Matthew Redman to outflank the Scots on his left.**

3. **PHASE TWO: The earl of Douglas approaches unseen by Hotspur due to the woods and undergrowth on the ridge. The Scottish flank attack surprises the disorganized English though they rally and a bloody melée ensues.**

4. **PHASE TWO: The English left wing under Redman attacks the Scottish servants' camp.**

5. **PHASE THREE: The arrival of the earl of March on the field tips the balance in favour of the Scots; although Douglas is killed his death goes unnoticed in the confusion.**

6. **PHASE THREE: A reinforcement of Scottish men-at-arms has not prevented Redman from taking the servants' camp.**

7. **Redman pursues defeated Scots' right wing up Redesdale.**

8. **Hotspur and his knights are defeated and surrender as the commons flee, though some elements of the English army withdraw in good order.**

66

REDMAN

THE BATTLE OF OTTERBURN, EARLY EVENING 5 AUGUST 1388

Note: Gridlines are marked at 1km/0.62 miles. Hill heights are given in brackets and measured in metres.

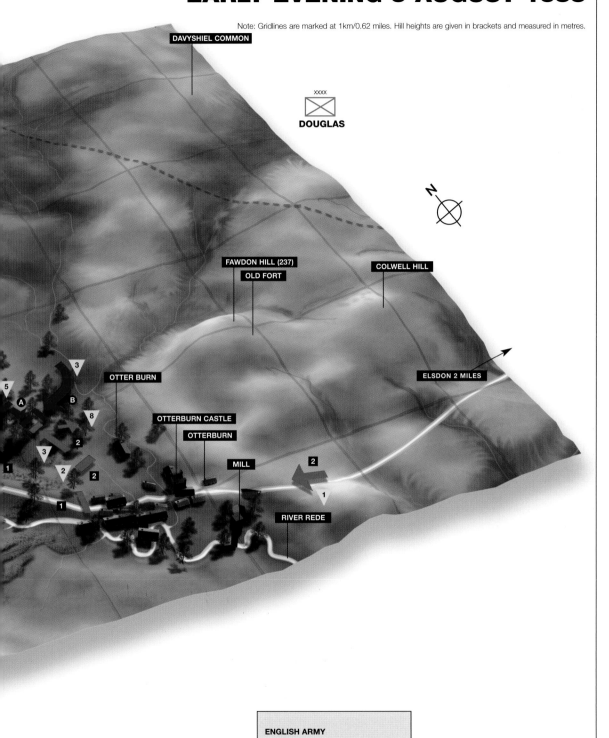

DAVYSHIEL COMMON

xxxx
DOUGLAS

FAWDON HILL (237)
OLD FORT

COLWELL HILL

N

ELSDON 2 MILES

OTTER BURN

3
5
A
B
8
2
3
2
2
1
1

OTTERBURN CASTLE
OTTERBURN
MILL

2
1

RIVER REDE

ENGLISH ARMY

1 Sir Matthew Redman's contingent
2 Hotspur's men-at-arms

Scottish Knights. From top left: Sir Robert Colville of Oxenham in Teviotdale; Sir Henry Preston of Craigmillar Castle in Midlothian; Sir Thomas Erskine of Alloa; Sir David Lindsay, Lord of Glenesk; Sir John Edmonstone, a knight of East Lothian; George Dunbar, Earl of March. We are fortunate that the Scottish section of the contemporary *Armorial de Gelre* includes the crests as well as the arms of many of the Scottish knights that fought at Otterburn. The curious beast on Sir John Edmonstone's helm is a camel. (Author's illustration, after Gelre)

As the twilight surrendered to the encroaching dark, the English men-at-arms, hardly able to lift their arms with fatigue, began to falter, and, gradually at first, as the pressure from the fresher Scottish troops bore inexorably down on them, they began to give way. As their formation disintegrated, shouts of triumph rang in their ears as the Scots, sensing victory, renewed their onslaught. The English line broke, and many fell beneath the thrusts of the Scottish spears, leaving a grim harvest of death in their bloody wake. The trickle to the rear of those who sought succour in flight became a torrent as the broken troops fled the fearful carnage for the safety of encroaching darkness. Many of the heavily armoured men-at-arms were too exhausted and encumbered by their armour to flee, and were captured; among them were Hotspur and his brother Ralph, who was badly wounded. The Westminster chronicler tells of the great slaughter among the English, of whom 'five hundred and fifty or more … perished'; amongst them were many of the town levies of Newcastle.

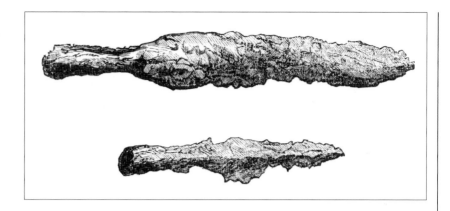

Robert White's 1857 *History of the Battle of Otterburn* includes these engravings of spearheads from Otterburn, which were found about 1816. According to White, pieces of swords, spears and the iron trappings of horses have been found on the battlefield. Mrs Buddle, a local woman, told him that part of a sword was found near the present cross but what became of it she did not know.

SUCCESS OF THE ENGLISH LEFT WING

But the fighting was not over with the defeat of the Percys; Wyntoun tells of a great commotion, coming from the direction of the Scottish camps. The Scots hastily despatched a body of men to investigate and they found numbers of the enemy still in the area of the servants' camp; they fell upon them, and killed all they found. These unfortunates can only have been stragglers from Redman's command. Redman himself, as the monk of Westminster relates with satisfaction,

> fought a very different battle [to Hotspur]. After reconnoitring the Scots he delivered an assault so resolute that they [the Scots] turned tail and he gave orders for every man of them to be killed with no quarter given except to those who could pay 100 marks for their helmets.

Redman pursued the fleeing Scots as far as the Scottish Border, 'dealing death and mortal wounds all the way'. It seems that Redman's troops, having successfully accomplished their part, rode far from the battlefield in pursuit of the fleeing Scots, killing the commons but taking prisoner those who would bring a good ransom, 'before returning home in triumph'.

One of the prisoners taken was Sir James Lindsay of Crawford, and his capture, if not the circumstance, is confirmed by Knighton and by surviving documentary evidence. Froissart relates in great detail how Lindsay fought and took Sir Mathew Redman prisoner, despatching him to Newcastle under parole before he was himself taken prisoner when he mistook his direction and blundered into the bishop of Durham's men in the darkness. However, contemporary records do not support Froissart's tale of Redman's capture; on the contrary, they suggest that he remained at liberty. Of the other leaders of the left wing, Sir Robert Ogle, according to Froissart, was similarly taken prisoner by the Scots; again, there is no evidence to confirm this. He was certainly at large in June 1389 when he and Sir Mathew Redman attacked the rearguard of a Scottish force returning from a raid into England. Sir Thomas Grey, Sir Thomas Umfraville and his brother Robert, it must be presumed, escaped capture, as there is no record to suggest otherwise. It is odd that the Umfravilles, despite their status as lords of Redesdale, are not

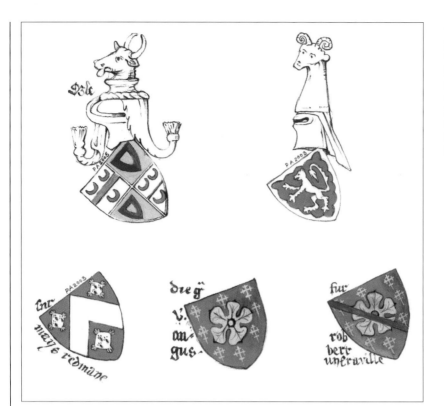

Leaders of the English left wing. From top left: Sir Robert Ogle of Ogle Castle in Northumberland; Sir Thomas Grey of Heton on the Till in Northumberland; Sir Mathew Redman of Levens Hall in Westmorland; Sir Thomas Umfraville, Lord of Redesdale; Sir Robert Umfraville, his brother. (Author's illustration)

mentioned in contemporary records, nor in any source other than Hardyng as having been at the battle of Otterburn, a state of affairs that has led to their presence at the battle being questioned.

Froissart tells how the Scots sustained most of their casualties as they pursued the English troops fleeing the battlefield: 'Of the Scots about a hundred were killed and two hundred taken prisoner in the pursuit when the English were retreating. If these saw an opportunity they turned back and fought with their pursuers. The only Scots to be captured were taken in this way, not in the battle.' This is not a description of a headlong disorderly flight; in fact it sounds as if a fair proportion of the English troops still had plenty of fight left in them, and made a fighting withdrawal. It is possible that there is some confusion in Froissart's account of the later stages of the battle, and that the casualties and prisoners that he tells of were those killed and captured by Sir Mathew Redman's command.

AFTERMATH

DEATH OF THE EARL OF DOUGLAS

But I have dream'd a dreary dream
Beyond the Isle of Skye;
I saw a dead man win a fight,
And I think that man was I.

Sir Walter Scott, The Battle of Otterburn

As dawn broke over the battlefield, the Scots discovered the earl of Douglas lying dead with his trusty esquires beside him. His impetuous bravery had led him to push too far into the ranks of the enemy, and he had paid the price for his failure to arm himself fully. He had been brought down by three spear wounds, in the shoulder, stomach and thigh; as he had fallen, his head had been cleaved with a battle axe. In the heat of battle the English had not realized that they had killed the earl of Douglas and his death had no influence on the outcome. In reality, it was not 'the dead Douglas' who won the battle of Otterburn; the true victor was George Dunbar, Earl of March.

THE BISHOP OF DURHAM MAKES A POOR SHOWING

The bishop of Durham arrived in Newcastle on the afternoon of the day of battle; after a brief rest he set out that very night to reinforce Hotspur. He had not covered two miles before men fleeing the battle told him that not only were they defeated, but the Scots were hard on their heels. When shortly afterwards crowds of fugitives poured down the road, the bishop's panicky troops turned and fled with them until he had not 500 left. The bishop himself returned to Newcastle where he managed to assemble a force, according to Froissart, of (incredibly) 10,000 men, with which he set out at sunrise. When they arrived at Otterburn, either that evening or the following day, the Scots were still in position in their camp; they had learned of the approach of the bishop's force and had elected to remain in Redesdale, secure in their strongly fortified position, because of the large numbers of prisoners and wounded that now encumbered them. As the lord bishop and his knights reconnoitred the enemy fortifications from a distance, the Scots, as was their habit, made a great din with a loud blowing of horns to unnerve the English and encourage their departure. It was soon decided, as the odds were against them, that this was indeed a suitable course of action, and the bishop drew off his men and rode back to Newcastle.

The monk of Westminster is highly critical of the conduct of the bishop of Durham, holding him partly responsible for the disaster that befell Hotspur. He thought that the bishop's force was near Otterburn at the time of the battle, and that the disaster could have been prevented, had it not been for the prelate's timidity. The truth is that, despite Froissart's exaggerated figures, the bishop's force was simply not strong enough to attack the Scots, and the bishop, knowing that a second defeat hard on the heels of the first would have been calamitous, prudently withdrew.

The black column of smoke that rose from their burning encampment signalled the Scots' withdrawal from Otterburn early the following morning. They took with them their captives and the bodies of the earl of Douglas and the Scottish knights who had been killed in the battle, and made their way unhurriedly towards the Border. The earl's closest companions conveyed his body by way of Dere Street, the old Roman Road that led to Melrose, where he was interred in a tomb alongside those of his ancestors in the ancient abbey of Melrose. When news of the battle of Otterburn reached the earl of Fife in the West March, he returned to Scotland by way of the Solway fords, taking a large number of captives with him. The Scots did not have things all their own way in the West March and many, according to Knighton, were killed and many more captured near Carlisle, 'taking to the water' – probably trapped by the speed of the incoming tides at the fords across the Solway.

The Scottish invasions of 1388 did a great deal of damage in the northern counties of England, and caused untold hardship, which was

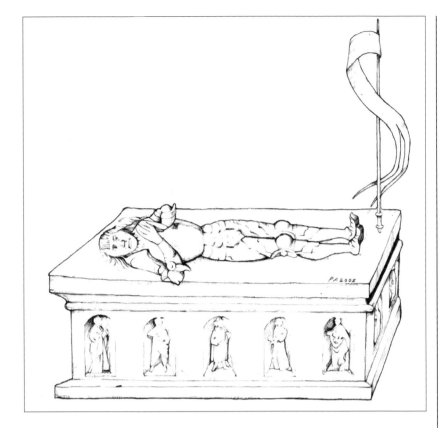

compounded by the ransoms that had to be found for the captives taken by the Scots. The battle of Otterburn was a humiliation for the English, made even more unpalatable by the capture of Hotspur, who was a popular national hero. At the great council of Northampton, held on 20 August, Scottish affairs were at the top of the agenda. New wardens were appointed to replace Hotspur and commissioners of array were instructed to levy troops for the defence of the Border. The king's plan to lead an immediate invasion of Scotland came to nothing, largely due to the huge expense of military undertakings on this scale. A truce was agreed between the English and French in June 1389, and the French insisted that the Scots be given the option of inclusion in this. Though opinion was sharply divided on the issue, the Scots decided to terminate hostilities and enter the Anglo-French truce themselves; thus the Otterburn War rather tamely petered out early in July 1389. The Scots' expectation that the military ascendancy they had gained over the English would force them to make peace on terms favourable to themselves, much as had occurred in 1327–28, had not been fulfilled. Apart from the ransoms from Otterburn, which were a valuable source of income for the Scots, the war resulted in little advantage to either side. What was seen as bungling, not only of the Scottish war, but also of the war in France, by the regime of the Lords Appellant, weakened their support and allowed Richard II and his faction to begin to re-establish their grip on power. One of the king's political successes was to win over the earl of Nottingham, who was sent to the north as warden of the East March. Early in 1389, when the earl of Fife and Sir Archibald Douglas attempted to repeat their invasion of the previous year, Nottingham outmanoeuvred them and

THE DEAD DOUGLAS IS BORNE AWAY BY HIS KNIGHTS AS THE VICTORIOUS SCOTS PREPARE TO RETURN HOME
(pages 74–75)

> Then on the morne they maye them beerys
> Of Byrch and haysell graye;
> Many a wydowe with wepyng teyres
> Ther makes they fette awaye.

'The Battle of Otterborne', from *Reliques of Ancient English Poetry*, 1794

Columns of acrid smoke rise from their burning encampment as the Scots, having seen off the bishop of Durham, prepare to return home. The bloodstained banner of the dead Douglas (1) serves as his winding sheet as he is borne on a wooden bier by six knights. Nearest of the group is Sir John Lindsay of Dunrod (2), in Renfrewshire. Froissart relates that when Douglas' banner bearer was killed and the earl himself lay mortally wounded, he ordered his banner to be raised again and 'The two brothers Sinclair and sir John Lindsay obeyed his orders.' The other identifiable knights in this group are Sir David Graham of Montrose (3), and Sir John Haliburton of Dirleton Castle in East Lothian (4); in June 1402 the English captured the latter at the combat of Nisbet Muir.

Watching the sad scene is a highland chieftain, armed in the manner of the West Highlands (5); at his side stands Sir Robert Colville of Oxenham in Teviotdale (6). When the Scots recovered Teviotdale from the English in 1384, Sir Robert returned to Scottish allegiance, forfeiting his lands in England. According to Froissart, Robert Colville and his sons John and Robert were knighted at Otterburn; he also tells of a valiant esquire named David Colville, 'an equal to the most eminent knights for courage and loyalty', who was killed bearing Douglas' banner. In the left foreground, Sir John Edmonstone (7) wipes away a tear; he was a knight of East Lothian and a staunch adherent of the Douglases who fought at Humbleton Hill in 1402 alongside the fourth earl. Beyond Sir John is the banner of Sir John Montgomery (8), Lord of Eaglesham, in Renfrewshire, who was the captor of Hotspur at Otterburn. Beyond Sir John's banner is that of Sir Henry Preston of Craigmillar Castle in Midlothian (9). He captured Sir Ralph Percy at Otterburn, a rich prize whose ransom was set at £900. His good fortune is confirmed by a charter of Robert III, dated 28 September 1390, detailing lands granted to 'Henry de Prestoun for the redemption of Sir Ranulph de Percy, Knight, Englishman'. In the centre is displayed the national flag of Scotland (10), which is of great antiquity and may have been the banner of the early kingdom of the Picts.

The picturesque fortified manor known as Aydon Castle, in Northumberland, was the home of Nicholas Reymes, an esquire who was captured at Otterburn. It is recorded that he was to receive 50 marks from the Crown 'in consideration of his great poverty as a result of the heavy ransom imposed by the Scots'. (Author's photo)

Ruins of Polnoon Castle, Ayrshire, said to have been built from the proceeds of Hotspur's ransom, a tradition supported by the fact that Polnoon derives from the Scots word *poind* – ransom. (Author's photo)

The shattered ruin of Ardrossan Castle stands high above the town; it was once the seat of Sir John Montgomery, Lord of Ardrossan, in Ayrshire. His capture of Hotspur at Otterburn earned him a rich reward in ransom money, though his fortunes were reversed at Humbleton Hill, after which he was a prisoner in England for at least a year, and paid a stiff price for his release. (Photo, Brian McGarrigle)

foiled their intentions. Though this time no battle was fought, it was clearly demonstrated to the Scots that the English recovery from the disaster of 1388 was complete, and that their determination to defend the Border was undiminished.

CASUALTIES AND CAPTIVES OF OTTERBURN

The casualty figures in the medieval sources are predictably exaggerated. Froissart is precise but unreliable; he says that on the English side 1,840 were slain, 1,000 badly wounded and 1,040 taken prisoner; on the Scots side a mere 100 were killed, and 200 taken prisoner, while pursuing the English. His information came from Scots who fought in the battle, which probably accounts for the astonishing imbalance of his figures. Walter Bower says only that 1,500 English were killed; he admits that many also fell on the Scottish side. The author of the *Orygynale Cronykil* was not sure what to believe; 'Sum sayis as thowsande deyd thare; Sum fyftene hundyr; and sum mare.' The Westminster chronicler's account of the battle suggests a more even contest, reflected by his casualty figures; he says that the Scots did 'tremendous slaughter among our men' and that 'five hundred and fifty or more ... perished by the edge of the sword.' This number he balances with the losses of the Scots, which he says were similar, amounting to over 500 killed 'in one area or the other'.

The evidence suggests that there were few if any fatalities among the small number of English knights who fought at Otterburn. Knighton tells us that Hotspur, his brother and 21 other knights were captured there but mentions no fatalities. We know 16 knights by name who took part in the battle, none of whom were killed in the fighting. The only death among the men of quality on record is that of an esquire whom Froissart names as Thomas Waltham; probably the same esquire named in an entry in the *Kirkstall Chronicle*: 'the warlike standard bearer of lord Henry Percy, called John Waltham ... fatally wounded he died at last.' Waltham, though obviously highly regarded, was not a knight, yet his death was considered important enough to be recorded by both Froissart and the Kirkstall chronicler. The fact that these well-informed sources mention only the death of an esquire at Otterburn suggests that there were no fatalities among the more noteworthy knights to record.

Apart from the earl of Douglas himself, whose death was partly due to his incomplete arming, fatalities among the Scots knights were similarly few, though we do know that Sir John Towers died of his wounds and that Sir Robert Hert was killed, both of whom formed part of the earl's retinue.

To some extent the remarkable durability of the knights can be attributed to the protection offered by the almost complete harness of plate armour that had developed by the 1380s, which was in general use by the knighthood of both sides at Otterburn. A heraldic surcoat, the prerogative of the knightly classes, was probably just as effective as a rich armour in ensuring survival; it was an indication that the bearer would bring a good ransom if taken alive. Practically all the English knights

ABOVE **The well-cared-for remains of the castle of Sir John Haliburton stand in the attractive East Lothian village of Dirleton. Sir John was an adherent of the Douglases and fought at Otterburn. He was defeated and captured at Nisbet Muir in 1402 by the earl of March. (Author's photo)**

RIGHT **Beneath the north wall of the church of St Cuthbert at Elsdon lie the remains of many of the English dead from the battle of Otterburn. The remains were discovered in the early 19th century during restoration work on the church, but have never been the subject of modern archaeological investigation. (Author's illustration)**

present seem to have been captured at Otterburn; when the tide of battle turned against them they would have been exhausted, encumbered by their armour, and having fought dismounted they were unable to escape. Having fought to the point where honour was satisfied, there was no shame in surrender, and the English knights seem to have been unanimous in preferring this to a heroic death in battle.

THE SITUATION IN SCOTLAND AFTER OTTERBURN

The death of the earl of Douglas restored the balance of losses at Otterburn to some degree, and made the battle a somewhat Pyrrhic victory for the Scots, for they had lost their most warlike leader. His death, without a legitimate successor, resulted in serious political upheaval over the question of succession. The title eventually went to the contender with the most political muscle: Archibald 'the Grim', Lord of Galloway, a natural son of 'the Good' Sir James Douglas, who became the third Earl of Douglas. The same upheaval left the earl of Fife, who had supported Archibald Douglas, as Lieutenant of Scotland, replacing his brother Carrick in that position. The death of James Douglas, and the political tensions that resulted, to some extent explain the failure of the Scots to follow up their victory at Otterburn. The truce signed in 1389 ended the war, and brought to nothing the Scottish attempt to force the English to agree a peace on their terms. Although the victory of Otterburn proved far from decisive, it marked the high point of one of the most successful periods in Anglo-Scottish warfare for the Scots, and symbolizes the successful conclusion of the Scottish Wars of Independence.

THE BATTLE OF HUMBLETON HILL, 14 SEPTEMBER 1402

SCOTLAND, 1389–1402

The years of truce that followed the conclusion of the Otterburn War brought an uneasy interlude of relative quiet to the turbulent Anglo-Scottish border, though this was punctuated by frequent cross-border violence that threatened the fragile peace. There was political turmoil in both England and Scotland in the years round the turn of the 14th century. In England, the usurper Henry Bolingbroke had been crowned as Henry IV in late 1399, in place of the deposed Richard II, who was subsequently murdered. Despite his insecure tenure of the throne, and beset by a multitude of problems, including unrest in Ireland, and the revolt of Owyn Glyndwr in Wales, Henry led a brief expedition into Scotland in 1400, perhaps urged by the political fruits to be gained from an easy victory, which would contrast with his predecessor Richard II's lack of success against the Scots. It was a fruitless expedition and did nothing to dent the confidence or aggression of the new Scottish leadership. In Scotland, King Robert II died in 1390, and was succeeded by his eldest son, John, Earl of Carrick, who styled himself Robert III. He left his eldest son David, Duke of Rothesay, to rule the kingdom, as he himself became increasingly ineffectual and marginalized. A power struggle between the heir to the throne and his uncle, the duke of Albany (formerly the earl of Fife), culminated in the seizure and disappearance of Rothesay, and allowed Albany to establish himself as ruler of Scotland.

Prominent among the new regime's supporters was Archibald, fourth Earl of Douglas, who had succeeded to the title on the death of his father, Archibald 'the Grim', in 1400. His thirst for military distinction led him to lend his backing to Albany, in return for free rein to indulge in war against England. Popular sentiment was in favour of this belligerent policy, which gave impetus to the warlike plans of the Scottish leadership. They were confident of their military prowess and pursued a provocative policy, which led to a deteriorating situation on the Anglo-Scottish border. When Douglas raided Northumberland, late in 1401, in flagrant violation of the peace agreement in force, a state of open warfare resulted. These events, together with the refusal of the Scots to enter into a truce in the winter of 1401–02, clearly signalled their intentions in the campaigning season ahead. The English government reacted vigorously and began to strengthen their border defences. The troops retained by the Crown in the Marches were alerted and paid at wartime rates: these included a force led by the Scottish earl of March, whose recent defection to English allegiance deprived the Scots of a leader of sound military judgement. It was a loss that they could ill afford.

The Scots suffered a defeat at the hands of the English defence forces in June 1402, when the earl of March intercepted a raiding party on its way home at Nisbet, in the Merse of Berwickshire, killing its leader, Sir Patrick Hepburn of Hailes, and taking prisoner several prominent knights of Lothian. It was a small affair, yet it should have signalled to Douglas the state of preparedness of the English troops on the Border and their fighting qualities.

The expected invasion was not launched until the beginning of September, when the Scottish army, possibly 10,000 strong, commanded by Archibald, Earl of Douglas and Murdoch Stewart, Earl of Fife, the feckless eldest son of the duke of Albany, invaded the East March, penetrating as far south as Newcastle. On their return northwards the Scots were surprised to find an English army drawn up in battle array across their route home, near Milfield, in the valley of the River Till, just north of Wooler, cutting off their retreat and placing them in a decidedly uncomfortable position. It was a situation that had the hallmark of careful planning on the part of the English leadership. The architects of the trap were the wily old earl of Northumberland; Hotspur, his associate commander; and the earl of March, whose counsel may have had a decisive influence on the strategy that had so neatly put the English in so advantageous a position.

The presence of the marauding Scots in Northumberland in September must have made it impossible for levies from the south to join the army at Milfield, at least by the direct route, though it is possible that English troops marched north before the invasion was launched and swelled the garrisons of the border castles until the trap was sprung. The need to concentrate troops from a wide area quickly suggests the

Arms and crests of Ralph, Baron of Greystoke, in Cumbria, and Sir Henry FitzHugh of Ravensworth, in North Yorkshire, who were among the English leaders at Humbleton Hill. From a contemporary report of the battle we know that also present were the earl of Northumberland; Sir Henry Percy (Hotspur); George Dunbar, Earl of March; William, Lord of Hilton; Sir Ralph Eure; Sir Robert Umfraville; and the keepers of the castles of Roxburgh and Dunstanburgh. (Author's illustration)

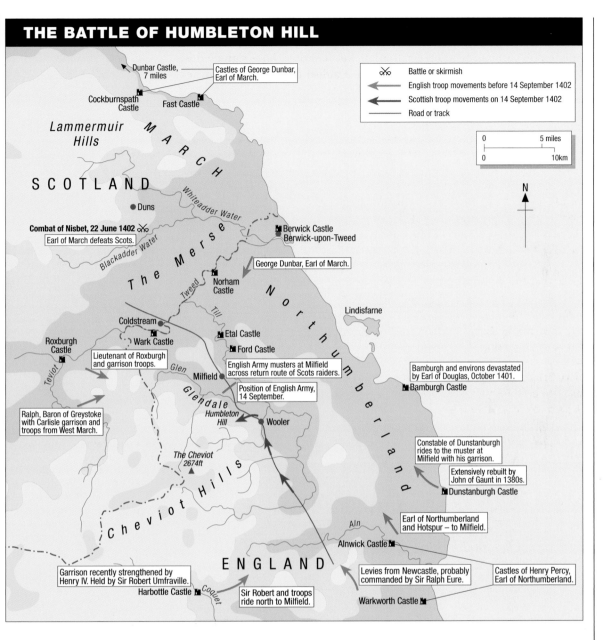

Dunbar Castle, 7 miles

Castles of George Dunbar, Earl of March.

Battle or skirmish

English troop movements before 14 September 1402

Scottish troop movements on 14 September 1402

Road or track

Cockburnspath Castle

Fast Castle

Lammermuir Hills

M A R C H

S C O T L A N D

Whiteadder Water

Duns

Combat of Nisbet, 22 June 1402
Earl of March defeats Scots.

Blackadder Water

Berwick Castle
Berwick-upon-Tweed

T h e   M e r s e

Tweed

George Dunbar, Earl of March.

Norham Castle

Till

Lindisfarne

N o r t h u m b e r l a n d

Coldstream

Wark Castle

Roxburgh Castle

Lieutenant of Roxburgh and garrison troops.

Glen

Etal Castle

Ford Castle

English Army musters at Milfield across return route of Scots raiders.

Bamburgh and environs devastated by Earl of Douglas, October 1401.

Bamburgh Castle

Teviot

Milfield

Position of English Army, 14 September.

Glendale

Humbleton Hill

Wooler

Ralph, Baron of Greystoke with Carlisle garrison and troops from West March.

Constable of Dunstanburgh rides to the muster at Milfield with his garrison.

Extensively rebuilt by John of Gaunt in 1380s.

Dunstanburgh Castle

The Cheviot 2674ft

C h e v i o t   H i l l s

Earl of Northumberland and Hotspur – to Milfield.

Aln

Alnwick Castle

E N G L A N D

Levies from Newcastle, probably commanded by Sir Ralph Eure.

Castles of Henry Percy, Earl of Northumberland.

Garrison recently strengthened by Henry IV. Held by Sir Robert Umfraville.

Harbottle Castle

Coquet

Sir Robert and troops ride north to Milfield.

Warkworth Castle

0   5 miles
0   10km

N

employment of large numbers of mounted men, both archers and men-at-arms. The lieutenant of Roxburgh Castle and the constable of Dunstanburgh Castle are known to have been present at Humbleton Hill with their garrison troops, and there were men from Carlisle, and no doubt from many another border stronghold, all well positioned to allow their garrisons to ride to Milfield without encountering the Scots in Northumberland.

Neither Archibald Douglas nor any of the Scottish leaders had an answer to their desperate plight, and even the famous Sir John Swinton seems to have been mesmerized by the situation. The Scots feared to face the massed English archers in open battle, so a decision was taken to climb the steep slopes of nearby Humbleton Hill and take up a defensive position within the tumbled ramparts of an old Iron Age fort that girded

LEFT, TOP **Humbleton Hill seen from the east with Coldberry Hill beyond. The Scots probably climbed Humbleton from this direction. The northern slopes are rough and broken by craggy outcrops, which can be seen on the right. (Author's photo)**

LEFT, BOTTOM **The *Historia Anglicana* tells us that some of the English climbed a hill opposite the Scots. This was probably Coldberry Hill, which is separated from the Scots' position on the summit of Humbleton Hill by a steep ravine. View north from the slopes of Coldberry Hill. (Author's photo)**

ABOVE **Humbleton Hill, on the left, is separated from Coldberry Hill by a deep ravine. English archers positioned on Coldberry would have commanded the southern slopes of Humbleton Hill. This is a view from the west. (Author's photo)**

the summit. Thus the Scots effectively cornered themselves, handing the initiative to the English, who advanced onto the lower slopes of the hill, closing the trap. According to Walter Bower, Hotspur urged an immediate charge by his knights and men-at-arms against the Scots on their hilltop, but was restrained by March, whose advice, to send the archers forward, prevailed. If the tale is true, it confirms that Hotspur was no more a competent military commander than the circumstances of his defeat at Otterburn suggest.

Humbleton Hill is just below 1,000ft (298m) in height; its steep upper slopes are littered with boulders and craggy outcrops, though there is easier ground in places, which would have afforded the English bowmen an approach to the Scottish position. Though it seems unlikely that they completely encircled the Scots, the archers would have had little difficulty in forming in large numbers within bowshot of them; they presented a large tempting target, for the confined rock-strewn top of Humbleton provided neither cover nor space to manoeuvre for so large a body of men. The murderous storm of arrows unleashed by the bowmen tore holes in the ragged formation of Scots, who soon began to break ranks and look for a way of escape rather than face the deadly arrow storm. Sir John Swinton kept his head however, and, mounting up as many knights and men-at-arms as would follow him, he led a desperate charge, in a last-ditch bid to break out of the trap. But it was hopeless; it was too late, for the vicious shafts of the encroaching bowmen flew on a flat trajectory now, piercing the jacks of the spearmen and punching through the armour of the men-at-arms. As the horsemen closed with the bowmen the intensity of their fire increased and the aim of every archer within range was drawn towards them; horses and men crashed to earth under a rain of steel that nothing could live through. Swinton and his brave hundred perished, and with them died the last hope of the remaining Scots, whose only thought now was of survival; they broke in rout and fled in any direction that seemed to offer an escape route. Because the hill was not completely encircled many of the broken Scots managed to escape the carnage of the battlefield, though pursuit of the fugitives was pressed remorselessly, and considerable numbers were drowned attempting to cross the River Tweed ten miles to the north.

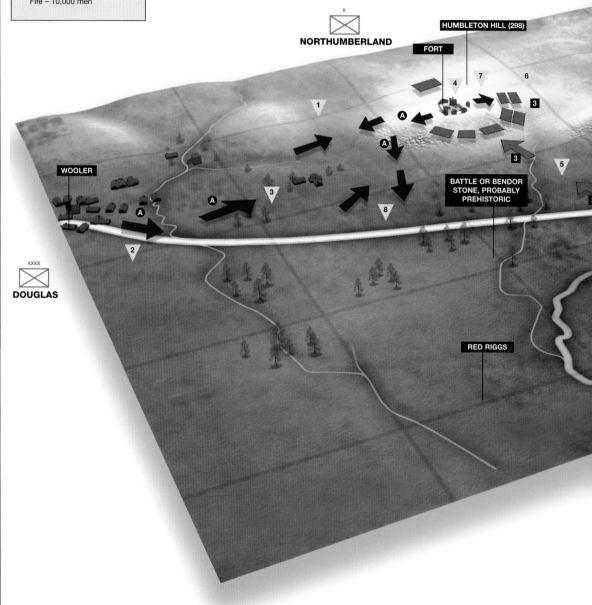

SCOTTISH ARMY

A Main Scottish army com-
manded by Archibald, fourth
Earl of Douglas and the earl of
Fife – 10,000 men

NORTHUMBERLAND

HUMBLETON HILL (298)

FORT

WOOLER

DOUGLAS

BATTLE OR BENDOR
STONE, PROBABLY
PREHISTORIC

RED RIGGS

THE BATTLE OF HUMBLETON HILL

14 September 1402 Hotspur revenges himself on the Douglases for his defeat at Otterburn.

Note: Gridlines are marked at 1km/0.62 miles. Hill heights are given in brackets and measured in metres.

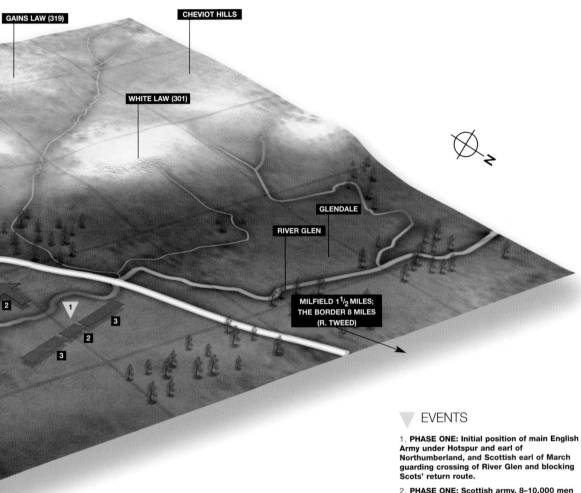

GAINS LAW (319)

CHEVIOT HILLS

WHITE LAW (301)

GLENDALE

RIVER GLEN

MILFIELD 1$\frac{1}{2}$ MILES; THE BORDER 8 MILES (R. TWEED)

ENGLISH ARMY

1 Main contingent of English army
2 Hotspur's men-at-arms
3 Dismounted English archers

▼ EVENTS

1. **PHASE ONE: Initial position of main English Army under Hotspur and earl of Northumberland, and Scottish earl of March guarding crossing of River Glen and blocking Scots' return route.**

2. **PHASE ONE: Scottish army, 8–10,000 men under earls of Douglas and Fife, realize that their route home is blocked.**

3. **PHASE ONE: Scots turn to Humbleton seeking a defensive position.**

4. **PHASE ONE: Scots crowded together *en schiltron* within tumbled ramparts of Iron Age fort.**

5. **PHASE TWO: Archers advance to bottom of Humbleton.**

6. **PHASE THREE: Main thrust of English attack launched by easiest approach to Scots position, up shallow valley onto west ridge.**

7. **PHASE THREE: Earl of Douglas leads last-ditch cavalry charge in attempt to break out.**

8. **PHASE FOUR: Scottish troops flee in disorder: many slain in Red Riggs, many more drown in River Tweed 10 miles north of Humbleton. Scots lords and knights save themselves by surrender.**

9. **PHASE FOUR: English knights and men-at-arms had no part in the fight but may have taken part in the pursuit.**

TOP **The long west ridge of Humbleton Hill was the scene of Sir John Swinton's ill-fated cavalry charge. Beyond the ridge is the valley of the River Till and on the left, behind White Law, are the hills above Flodden, scene of a later and equally disastrous Scottish defeat. (Author's photo)**

RIGHT **The 'Bendor Stone' stands in an area below Humbleton Hill known as 'Red Riggs', where many of the Scots attempting to flee the battle were killed. The stone is probably an ancient standing stone or the last remnant of a circle that has become associated with the battle. (Author's photo)**

TOP **The west ridge of Humbleton Hill provides an easy ascent route, and was the scene of Sir John Swinton's cavalry charge. On the left is the deep ravine that separates Humbleton from Coldberry Hill. (Author's photo)**

ABOVE **Glendale and the valley of the River Till looking north, towards Milfield and Flodden Edge beyond, from the Scottish position on Humbleton Hill. The stones in the foreground mark the outer perimeter of the ancient hill fort. (Author's photo)**

Apart from Sir John Swinton, and the lord of Graham, there were few Scottish knights of note among the heaps of slain that littered the bloodsoaked summit of Humbleton Hill; as usual it was the commons who suffered most. The fighting had barely lasted an hour, yet the profits were great, as there was a rich haul of prisoners whose ransoms would turn around the fortunes of many an impoverished English knight and esquire. Five earls, including Douglas and Murdoch Stewart, and over 100 Scottish lords and knights were captured that day; it was a tally from which the scale of the disaster can be gauged. It was revenge indeed for Hotspur's reverse at Otterburn, for at Humbleton Hill Scotland suffered one of her worst defeats.

Archibald Douglas was not one of Scotland's great military commanders, as both his subsequent career and his cognomen, 'the Tyneman', or loser, amply confirm. His tactical response to the trap that Hotspur set outside Wooler led the Scots to disaster on Humbleton Hill. Nevertheless, his qualities as a fighting man cannot be denied; he had been in the thick of the action and, despite the protection of an armour so rich as to excite the comments of the chroniclers, was wounded in five places and lost an eye.

EPILOGUE

The battle of Humbleton Hill, far from setting the seal on the Percys' position of power, proved to be the pivot on which their fortunes turned; thereafter their restless ambition, fuelled by real and imagined grievances, led to their already strained relations with the king deteriorating dramatically. From a Scottish perspective the defeat at Humbleton awakened fears of a renewed occupation of southern Scotland, or even of another attempt at conquest. Henry IV granted to the Percys all the lands of the captured earl of Douglas, and promised the earl of March restoration of his lost lands across the Border. This incentive to re-conquest prompted Hotspur to lead his forces into Scotland in 1403, to take possession of Douglas' lands. Early in July, in pursuit of his territorial ambitions, Hotspur was engaged in the siege of Cocklaw Castle in Roxburghshire, when tensions between the Percys and the king spilled over into full-scale rebellion. Hotspur, with about 200 men, including Archie Douglas and other Scottish prisoners from Humbleton, who it seems threw in their lot with Percy in return for their freedom, left Cocklaw and rode south towards the Border, heading for Chester to raise an army to confront the king.

Hotspur was defeated and killed at the battle of Shrewsbury on 21 July, 1403. His body was taken by his kinsman Thomas Neville, Lord Furnival, and buried at Whitchurch, some 16 miles north of the battlefield. However, in order to scotch rumours that Hotspur still lived, the king had his body brought back to Shrewsbury, where it was salted and erected between two millstones beside the pillory in the main street. After some days the body was cut up; the head was sent to adorn one of the gates of York; the quarters to hang above the gates of London, Bristol, Chester and Newcastle. The rebellious old earl of Northumberland himself managed to soldier on until 1406, when he was killed on Bramham Moor, once more in rebellion against Henry IV's loathsome regime. At one time there were monuments to both Hotspur and his father in York Minster; their effigies stood on the right hand of the high altar, but neither has survived. However, no matter – Shakespeare has ensured Hotspur's immortality:

> … and by his light
> Did all the chivalry of England move
> To do brave acts. He was indeed the glass
> Wherein the noble youth did dress themselves.
>
> Shakespeare, *Henry IV Part II*

The Percy rebellion of 1403 was a serious threat to Henry IV's tenure of the throne and distracted him from his involvement in Scottish affairs. A chronic shortage of cash, and the renewal of French pressure

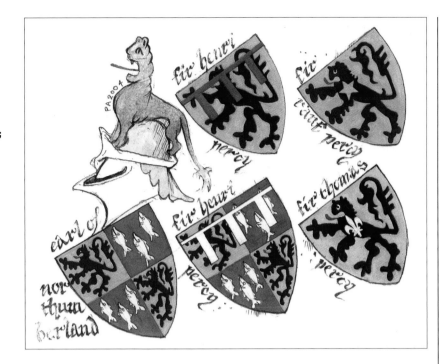

Arms of the Percys. The crest is that of the earl of Northumberland, below which is his shield, bearing the quartered arms of Percy and Lucy. The other shields, clockwise from the top, are: Hotspur until 1399; Sir Ralph Percy, his brother; Sir Thomas Percy, Earl of Worcester; Hotspur from 1399–1403 – though the colour of the label is uncertain. (Author's illustration)

on English possessions in France, shifted the focus of Henry's attention elsewhere, allowing the Scots a breathing space in which to recover from the disaster at Humbleton; in effect the Anglo-Scottish Wars petered out. In 1424, during one of England's most successful periods of the Hundred Years War, Archibald Douglas brought a Scottish army to France to confront the English in battle once more. In return, the French, having an exaggerated regard for his military prowess, created him Duke of Touraine and gave him high command. In August 1424, Douglas had his wish, and the confident Scots, along with their more wary French allies, gave battle to the English forces commanded by the duke of Bedford outside Verneuil. It was a hard-fought battle, but ultimately the French wing of the combined army gave way and left the Scots in the lurch; Douglas was killed in the ensuing carnage of defeat, along with the flower of the Scottish expeditionary force.

THE BATTLEFIELDS TODAY

The traditional site of the battle of Otterburn is to be found about a mile north-west of the village of the same name. In a coppice by the roadside, on the lower slopes of Blakeman's Law, stands the recently renovated Percy's Cross; this and a nearby notice board are the only indicators of the battlefield. Hotspur probably launched his attack from near this point, and, though there would have been more woodland in his day, the battlefield remains much as it would have been in the 14th century. Just over a mile to the north-west, situated within the bounds of the Northumberland National Park, is the summit of Blakeman's Law, 860ft (274m); the main fighting took place on the lower slopes of the broad ridge that leads down from there towards Otterburn. About half a mile beyond Percy's Cross stands the farm of Greenchesters, where the Scots built a fortification across the road up Redesdale, to safeguard the plundered livestock and their horses, which were turned loose in the flat valley bottom where the River Rede loops south below the farm. An unfenced, gated road leads past the farm and climbs steeply up Blakeman's Law, passing close beneath the summit. The flat shoulder

The windswept site of the battle of Otterburn remains unspoiled amid fine open countryside. The upper slopes of Blakeman's Law offer a wide prospect of Redesdale and the battlefield; on the hillside the remains of old coppices suggest the former more abundant medieval vegetation. (Author's photo)

ABOVE **Percy's Cross was erected in 1777 by the local landowner in a position close to the new turnpike road up Redesdale, where it could be admired by passing travellers. A new pedestal was built and the socket of the old 'Battle Stone' was set into the top of this to support an obelisk. This was actually an old stone lintel from Otterburn Hall that formed the upright shaft that, when topped with a pointed stone, finished the monument at 'a trifling expense'. (Author's illustration)**

ABOVE, RIGHT **A Victorian gothic edifice has replaced the medieval tower of the Umfravilles in Otterburn; a shield over the doorway bears their arms and serves as a reminder of the loss of the old fortress. (Author's photo)**

below, to the south-east, overlooks Redesdale and was the location of the camp of the Scottish knights and men-at-arms. A few hundred yards south-west of the top of Blakeman's Law stand the remains of the pele of Shittlehaugh, in a location offering a fine prospect of the surrounding area. The ruins have an evocative medieval aura, though it is unlikely that the present fabric existed in Hotspur's time. The Iron Age fort on Blakeman's Law is marked on the OS sheet as a 'Homestead', but is not easy to find on the ground. It is possible to make out a depression in the landscape, on the flat shoulder, lying more or less east to west, which may have played a part in the concealment of Douglas' movement onto the flank of Hotspur's advance. The site of the men-at-arms' camp provides the finest viewpoint of the battlefield as a whole, and a walk around this area unfolds a panorama from which the events of the battle can be recreated in the mind's eye. Three hundred feet below, the silver ribbon of the River Rede snakes along the valley floor, and a narrow dark green strip above the main road, three-quarters of a mile away, marks the position of Percy's Cross. Looking down the ridge, it is quite clear that it must have been trees and vegetation, rather than the profile of the ridge, that afforded concealment to the Scots, and enabled them to take Hotspur's force in flank, somewhere above the site of the cross.

The road to Humbleton Hill from Otterburn meanders for 50 miles, on both sides of the border, through some of the most delightful scenery that Britain has to offer. Humbleton Hill forms the north-eastern bastion of the Cheviot Hills, rising in a series of steepening steps above Glendale, near Wooler. The hill stands within the Northumberland National Park, and is separated from the main block of the Cheviots by a steep ravine, from which the name Humbleton, meaning 'cleft hill', is derived. There is a popular walkers' trail from Wooler, which can be followed to the top of Humbleton, where the tumbled ramparts of an ancient hill fort define the defensive position taken up by Douglas' army. A perambulation of the summit provides fine views over the Cheviots and along the valley of the River Till, which flows north to join the River Tweed, marking the borderline 12 miles away. At the base of the hill, to the north, just beyond the main road, stands the 'Bendor Stone', where many of the fleeing Scots were cut down in the area known as 'Red Riggs'. There are no signs to mark the battlefield; it remains unchanged, much as it was on that deadly September afternoon over 600 years ago.

SELECT BIBLIOGRAPHY

Archibald 'the Grim' founded Lincluden College, in Kirkcudbrightshire, towards the end of the 14th century. In 1400 he was succeeded by his son Archibald, fourth Earl of Douglas, called 'the Tyneman', who was killed in 1424 at the battle of Verneuil and buried in the cathedral of Tours. Lincluden had been intended as the burial place of both the earl and his wife Margaret, daughter of Robert III; in the event, only the widowed Princess Margaret was interred here. The building is enriched not only by her magnificent tomb, but by a series of carvings of the heraldry of the Douglases and the families with which they were connected. (Author's photo)

Primary Sources

Bain, J., ed., *Calendar of Documents relating to Scotland*, Edinburgh (1881–88)
Barry, Thomas, untitled poem, included in the *Scotichronicon*
Bower, Walter, *Scotichronicon*, Vol. 7, ed. D.E.R. Watt, Aberdeen (1996)
Froissart, Jean, *Chronicles of England*, France, etc., various editions
Gelre, *Armorial de Gelre* (Scottish section *c.*1385), Louvain (1992)
Hardyng, J., *The Chronicle of John Hardyng* (extract included in R. White)
Knighton, Henry, *Leycestrensis Chronicon*, Rolls Series
Walsingham, Thomas, *Historia Anglicana*, Rolls Series
Westminster Chronicle 1381–1394, Oxford (1982)
Wyntoun, Andrew, *The Origynale Cronykil of Scotland*, eds. Edmonstone and Douglas, Edinburgh (1872–79)

Secondary Sources

Armstrong, P., *The Battle of Otterburn 1388*, Lynda Armstrong Designs Pubs, Keswick (2003)
Boardman, A.W., *Hotspur*, Sutton Press, Stroud (2003)
Brown, Michael, *The Black Douglases*, Tuckwell Press, East Linton (1998)
Campbell, Colin, *The Scots Roll*, The Heraldry Society of Scotland, Scotland (1995)
Foster, J., *Some Feudal Coats of Arms*, James Parker and Co., Oxford (1902)
Heath, Ian, *Armies of the Middle Ages* vol.1, Wargames Research Group, Devizes (1982)
Macdonald, Alastair J., *Border Bloodshed*, Tuckwell Press, East Linton (2000)
MacDonald, W.R., *Scottish Armorial Seals*, Wm Green, Edinburgh (1904)
Maclean-Eltham, B., *Heraldry of Cumbria*, Kendal (1990)
Nicholson, Ranald, *Scotland, The Later Middle Ages*, Mercat Press, Edinburgh (1974)
Pease, Howard, *The Lord Wardens of the Marches*, Constable, London (1913)
Pinches R. and A. Wood, *A European Armorial c.1425–66*, (1971)
Redesdale Society (eds.), *The Battle of Otterburn*, Hindson Print, Newcastle-upon-Tyne (1988)
Robson, James, *Border Battles and Battlefields*, J and JH Rutherford, Kelso (1897)
Scott-Giles, C.W., *Shakespeare's Heraldry*, (London, 1950)
Surtees, R., *The History and Antiquities of the County Palatinate of Durham*, London (1816–40)
Tuck, A., and Goodman A. (eds) *War and Border Societies in the Middle Ages*, London (1992,)
Wesencraft, C., *The Battle of Otterburn*, Athena Books, (1988)
White, R., *History of the Battle of Otterburn*, Newcastle, (1857)
Willement, Thomas (ed.), *A Roll of Arms of the Reign of Richard II*, London, (1834)

INDEX

Figures in **bold** refer to illustrations

Albany, duke of *see* Fife and Menteith, Robert Stewart, Earl of
Alnwick Castle **11**
Angus, Archibald Douglas, Earl of 73
Appleby 37
archers
    English mounted 27–8, **27**
    at Humbledon Hill (1402) 83–5
    longbows **27**
    Scottish 24
Archibald 'the Grim' *see* Douglas, Sir Archibald
Ardrossan Castle **78**
armour
    aventails **28**
    padded **23**, **27**
    plate **24**, **25**, **28**, **29**
    plate gauntlets **27**
    poleyns **29**
    protective qualities 78
Arundel, earl of 11, 13
Athol, Aymer de **48**
Aydon Castle **77**

Balliol, Edward, King of Scots 8, **8**, 29
Balliol, John, King of Scots **7**
banners **62–4**, **74–6**
Bannockburn, battle of (1314) 29
Barry, Thomas 52, 56, 57
Beaumont, Henry de 29
Berwick-upon-Tweed 9, 26
Boroughbridge, battle of (1322) 29
Bower, Walter
    background 52
    on casualties 78
    on Humbleton Hill (1402) 85
    on Otterburn (1388) 18, 27, 32, 37–8, 64, 65
bows *see* archers
Brough Castle 37, **37**
'Burnt Candlemas' campaign (1356) 9

Carlingford **31**, 32
Carlisle 36–7
    castle **11**, 12
    West Walls **36**
Carrick, John Stewart, Earl of (later Robert III) 13, 16, 34, 81
    arms and crest **18**
cavalry *see* knights; men-at-arms
Cavers Ensign **51**
Clifford, Sir Thomas 17
clothing
    jupons **29**
    surcoats **27**
Cockermouth Castle **10**
Colville, David 76
Colville, Sir John 76

Colville, Sir Robert **74–6**
    arms and crest **68**
commission of array 26
Copledyke, Sir John **62–4**
Corbeil, Treaty of (1326) 8

David II, King of Scots 8–9
Delaval, Sir Raymond 47
Dirleton Castle **79**
Douglas and Mar, James, second Earl of 17
    arms and crest **18**
    burial 72, **73**
    death **62–4**, 65, 71, **74–6**, 78
    death's legacy 80
    duel with Hotspur **42–4**, 45–7
    friction with Percys 13
    and Otterburn campaign (1388) 23, 32, 34–6, 37–45
    at Otterburn (1388) 50, 53, 57
    standards **51**
Douglas, Archibald, third Earl of *see* Douglas, Sir Archibald
Douglas, Archibald, fourth Earl of ('the Tyneman')
    at Humbleton Hill (1402) 82, 83, 89, 90
    at Verneuil (1424) 91, 94
Douglas, Sir Archibald ('the Grim') 17, 36, 73–8, 80, 81, 94
Douglas, Archibald (son of earl of Douglas) 51
Douglas, Sir James ('the Good') 18, 80
Douglas, Sir William 17, 37
Dunbar, George, tenth Earl of Dunbar and third Earl of March 17–18
    arms and crest **68**
    goes over to English 19, 90
    at Humbleton Hill (1402) 17–18, 19–20, 81, 82, 85
    and Otterburn (1388) 38, 65–8, 71
Dunbar Castle **19**
Dundonald Castle **16**
Dupplin Muir, battle of (1332) 8, 29
Durham, lord bishop of (either Fordham or Skirlaw) 21, 26, 48, 56, 71–2

Edinburgh, Treaty of (1328) 8
Edlingham Castle **72**
Edmonstone, Sir John **74–6**
    arms and crest **68**
Edward I, King of England 29
Edward II, King of England 7, 29
Edward III, King of England 7–9, 29
Elsdon: church of St Cuthbert **79**
England
    Douglas' invasion of East March *see* Otterburn campaign
    Fife's invasion of West March 13, 23, 32, 36–7, **35**, 72
English army 25–30

commanders 19–21
order of battle 30
plans 32–3
strength 26–7
tactics 29–30
equipment: Scottish army 23
Erskine, Sir Thomas **62–4**
    arms and crest **68**
esquires 28
Etchingham, Sir William **28**
Eure, Sir Ralph (sheriff of Newcastle) 26, 82
Eure, Sir Ralph (under Henry VIII) 73

Falkirk, battle of (1298) 29
Felbrigge, Sir George **29**
Felton, Sir John 72
Fife, Murdoch Stewart, Earl of 82, 89
Fife and Menteith, Robert Stewart, Earl of (later Duke of Albany) 17
    arms and crest **18**
    invasion of West March (1388) 13, 23, 32, 36–7, **35**, 72
    later power struggles 80, 81
    new invasion attempted (1389) 73–8
Fitzhugh, Sir Henry: arms and crest **82**
Fordham, John *see* Durham, lord bishop of
France
    'auld alliance' 8–9
    and Hundred Years War 12, 91
    invasion of England (1385) 9
    truce with England (1389) 73
Froissart, Jean
    background 51
    on bishop of Durham 72
    on casualties 78
    on Douglas-Hotspur duel 44, 45
    informants 28, 51
    on Otterburn (1388) 19, 51, 52, 53, 60, 61, 65, 69, 70, 76
    on Otterburn campaign (1388) 22, 23, 26, 33, 34, 48, 56
    on Percy-Neville relations 10–11
Furnival, Thomas Neville, Lord 90

Gilbert of Grenlaw **24**, **25**
Graham, Sir David **74–6**
Grey, Sir Thomas 45, 69
    arms and crest **70**
Greystoke, Ralph, Baron of **20**
    arms and crest **82**

Haliburton, Sir John, of Dirleton Castle **74–6**, 79
Hallidon Hill, battle of (1333) 8, 29
Harcla, Andrew de 29
Hardyng, John 20–1, 49, 51, 57, 70
helmets
    bascinets **27**
    crested helms **18**, **25**, **26**, **68**, **70**, **82**

Henry IV, King of England 81, 90–1
Hepburn, Sir Patrick **62–4**, 82
Hermitage Castle **36**
Hert, Sir Robert 78
Highlanders 24, **74–6**
Hilton, Sir Thomas 64
Hilton, Sir William **62–4**
Holm Cultram Abbey 13
horses: value 27–8
Hotspur (Sir Henry Percy) 19–20, **26**
   appointed warden of East March 10, 13
   arms **91**
   crest **26**
   duel with Douglas **42–4**, 45–7
   at Humbleton Hill (1402) 19–20, 82, 85
   military competence 85
   at Otterburn (1388) 57, 61, 68, 73, 76, 78
   and Otterburn campaign (1388) 20, 41, **42–4**, 45–7, 48–9, 56–7
   personal retinue 26
   rebellion and death 20, 90
Humbleton Hill, battle of (1402) 17–18, 19–20, 81–9, **83**
   Border Stone **88**
   site **84, 85, 88, 89**, 93

Ireland, Scottish attack on (1388) 31, 32, 33, **35**, 37
Irish warriors **33**
Isabella, Queen of England 7–8
Isle of Man, Scottish attack on (1388) 31, 32, **35**, 37

James I, King of Scots 19
Jedburgh Castle 34

Kirkstall Chronicle 78
Knighton, Henry 51, 52, 69, 72, 78
knights
   arms and crests **18, 68, 70, 82**
   English 28, **28, 29**
   Scottish 24, **24, 25**

levying troops 22–3, 25–6
Lilburn, Sir John **62–4**
Lincluden College **94**
Lindsay, David, Lord of Glenesk: arms and crest **68**
Lindsay, Sir James 19, 69
Lindsay, Sir John **74–6**
Lochmaben Castle 9, **10**
Lucy family arms **10**
Lucy, Maud de 14
Lumley, Sir Ralph 45

March, earl of *see* Dunbar, George, tenth Earl of Dunbar and third Earl of March
Marches and March wardens 25
Margaret, Princess, Countess of Douglas 94
Margaret of Mar 18
men-at-arms
   English 28, **28**
   Scottish 23, 24
'Merciless Parliament' 9
Montgomery, Sir John, Lord of Eaglesham and Ardrossan 76, 78
Moray, John Dunbar, first Earl of 18, 38, 57, **62–4**, 65
Mortimer, Roger 7–8
Multon family arms **10**

Neville family
   arms **10**
   relations with Percy family 10
Neville, John, Lord 19
Neville, Margaret 14
Neville's Cross, battle of (1346) 9, 16, 28
Newcastle-upon-Tyne
   castle **49**
   defences 32, **42–4, 45**
   and Otterburn campaign (1388) 26, 41, **42–4**, 45–7
Nisbet Muir, combat of (1402) 82
Northumberland, Henry Percy, Earl of 14, 19, 82, 90
   arms 14, **91**
Nottingham, Thomas Mowbray, Earl of 18, 25, 27, 73–8

Ogle, Sir Robert 19, 20, 45, 69
   arms and crest **70**
orders of battle 30
Orygynale Cronykil (Wyntoun) *see* Wyntoun, Andrew
Otterburn, battle of (1388) 51–70
   aftermath 71–8, 80
   battlefield markers **65**
   burial place of English **79**
   casualties and captives 78–80
   date 52–3
   medieval written sources 51–2
   site 52, **52, 55, 56, 60, 61**, 92–3, **92**
Otterburn campaign (1388)
   Douglas' invasion 23, 32, 34–6, 37–45, **35, 39**
   Hotspur pursues Scots 48–9
   role in Scottish plans 32, 34–6, 37–8
   Scots before Newcastle 45–7
   Scots withdraw to Otterburn 47–8, **54**
Otterburn Castle 49–50, 72, **93**
Ottercops Hill **40**

pay: horse archers 28
Percy family
   arms **10, 14, 91**
   friction with Douglases 13
Percy, Sir Henry *see* Hotspur
Percy, Sir Ralph 20, **62–4**, 68, 76
   arms **91**
Percy's Cross **92, 93**
Polnoon Castle **77**
Ponteland 47, 48
Preston, Sir Henry 76
   arms and crest **68**
Prudhoe Castle **12, 46**

Radcot Bridge, battle of (1388) 9, 19
Ramsay, Sir Alexander **25**
recruitment *see* levying troops
Redeswire 38, **38**
Redman, Sir Mathew **19**, 20
   arms and crest **70**
   and Berwick 26
   Hardyng on 21
   and Otterburn (1388) 45, 57, 69, 70
Reliques of Ancient English Poetry 34, 38, 76
Reymes, Nicholas 77
Richard II, King of England 19
   death 81
   invasion of Scotland (1385) 9, 19
   and Otterburn's aftermath 73–4
   political situation 9, 19, 31, 73
   war preparations 13, 36–7, 41–5

Robert I (the Bruce), King of Scots 7–8, **7**, 11, 18, 29, 31
Robert II, King of Scots 9, 16, 34, 81
   arms and crest **18**
Robert III, King of Scots *see* Carrick, John Stewart, Earl of
Rothesay, David Stewart, Duke of 81
Rothley Crags **40, 41**

Scotichronicon (Bower) *see* Bower, Walter
Scotland **6**
   Hotspur's invasion (1403) 90
   Richard II's invasion (1385) 9, 19
   Royal Arms **7**
Scott, Sir Walter 53, 71
Scottish army 22–5
   commanders 16–18
   muster 34–6
   order of battle 30
   plans 31–2
   strength 23–4, 27
   tactics 24–5
shields: bucklers **27**
Shrewsbury, battle of (1403) 18, 20, 90
Skirlaw, Walter *see* Durham, lord bishop of
Southdean 32
spears and spearmen **23**, 24, 69
Stewart family: arms and crests **18**
Stewart, Sir Robert 18, 37
strategy
   English 25, 32–3
   Scottish 25, 31–2
Swinton, Sir John 18
   experience 24
   at Humbleton Hill (1402) 83, 85, 88, 89
   at Otterburn (1388) **62–4**, 65
swords 24, 25

tactics 24–5, 29–30
Threave Castle 17, **17**
Tilliol, Peter de 37
Towers, Sir John 78
travel speeds, medieval armies 22, 28, 36, 41

Umfraville family arms **10**
Umfraville, Sir Robert 20–1, 69–70, 82
   arms and crest **70**
Umfraville, Sir Thomas 20–1, 69–70
   arms and crest **70**

Vere, Robert de 9, 19
Verneuil, battle of (1424) 91
Vienne, Jean de 9

Walsingham, Thomas 51, 52, 65, 85
Waltham, Thomas or John 78
Warkworth Castle **46, 47**
Weardale campaign (1327) 29
Westminster Chronicle
   on bishop of Durham 72
   on Hotspur-Douglas relations 45–7
   on Otterburn (1388) 20, 53, 57, 68, 78
   overview as source 51
   on Scottish army 23
White, Robert 69
William, Lord of Hilton 82
Worcester, Sir Thomas Percy, Earl of: arms **91**
Wyntoun, Andrew 27, 52, 57, 60–1, 64, 69, 78

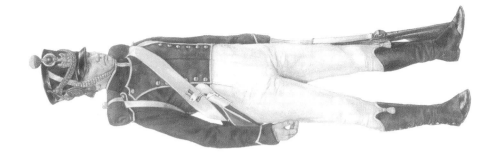

FIND OUT MORE ABOUT OSPREY

❏ Please send me the latest listing of Osprey's publications

❏ I would like to subscribe to Osprey's e-mail newsletter

Title / rank

Name

Address

City / county

Postcode / zip   state / country

e-mail

CAM

I am interested in:

❏ Ancient world   ❏ American Civil War
❏ Medieval world   ❏ World War 1
❏ 16th century   ❏ World War 2
❏ 17th century   ❏ Modern warfare
❏ 18th century   ❏ Military aviation
❏ Napoleonic   ❏ Naval warfare
❏ 19th century

Please send to:

North America:
Osprey Direct, c/o Random House Distribution Center,
400 Hahn Road, Westminster, MD 21157, USA

UK, Europe and rest of world:
Osprey Direct UK, P.O. Box 140, Wellingborough,
Northants, NN8 2FA, United Kingdom

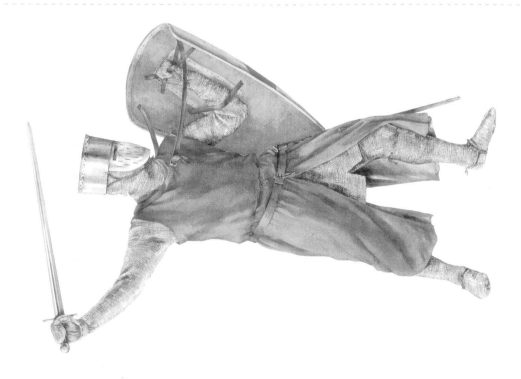

OSPREY
PUBLISHING

Young Guardsman
Figure taken from Warrior 22:
Imperial Guardsman 1799–1815
Published by Osprey
Illustrated by Richard Hook
www.ospreypublishing.com

Knight, c.1190
Figure taken from Warrior 1: *Norman Knight 950 - 1204 AD*
Published by Osprey
Illustrated by Christa Hook

POSTCARD